Dear Gloria;
    Do hope you enjoy reading
this book. Jeannette McCall

THE FIRST AND LAST BELL

A STORY OF SIX MISSIONS FOR BLACKS IN WILCOX COUNTY, ALABAMA

JEANNETTE STEELE MCCALL

American Literary Press
Baltimore, Maryland

The First and Last Bell

Library of Congress
Cataloging-in-Publication Data
ISBN 1-56167-909-7

Library of Congress Card Catalog Number:
2005905425

Published by

American Literary Press

8019 Belair Road, Suite 10
Baltimore, Maryland 21236

Manufactured in the United States of America

DEDICATION

This book is dedicated to the loving memory of my parents, Mr. Noy and Mrs. Hattie Roberta Watkins Steele, whose guidance, love for God, their children and education inspired and motivated their children to become the best that they could be.

Acknowledgements

There were numerous individuals and a lot of research that helped to make this account possible. Great effort has gone into making this exposition as factual as possible. Several books and many writings of various lengths about the United Presbyterian Missions have been written but to my knowledge no book has surfaced which contains a compiled story of the six missions.

Very special thanks are extended to all the individuals who shared their information with me by interviews, telephone calls, letters and written materials. Mrs. Alberta Thomas, Mrs. Izola Gailes, two sisters, Mmes. Evie Marshall Hall and Mrs. Ora D. Marshall Hicks, Mrs. and Mrs. James Ephraim, Jr., Mrs. Maggie Brown, my three sisters Mrs. Hattie Irene Steele Hayes, Mrs. Gertrude Edna Steele Arnett and Mrs. Willie Agnes Steele Coleman, Mr. Johnny Southhall, Miss Sadie Jackson and her brother Mr. Leroy Jackson.

Other materials for this story were collected from the following sources:

1. Minutes of the Wilcox County Board of Education Meetings
2. Certain excerpts from *Beginnings in the Black Belt and Short Stories of the Lives of Dr. Charles Henry and Mrs. Tillie E. Johnso*n by Sophia Cox Johnson
3. *Writings on Arlington Literary and Industrial High School* by Mrs. Naomi Fisher Hawkins

In addition, old records and minutes from Arlington, Miller's Ferry and Prairie provided some information.

CONTENTS

FOREWORD

On a particular morning in 1884, a mission bell peeled out the message to the Miller's Ferry community that the door of an old log church was open for school. Miss Henrietta Mason became the first teacher to open a mission school for black boys and girls in very, very rural Wilcox County.

Surely there must have been a great smile on the young teacher's face as she watched the boys and girls file into the little, one-room school building for the first time—some perhaps small in size for their age, some overgrown, and others just the right size for their ages. It was the young teacher's first assignment and the children's first opportunity to attend school.

With an excited group of black boys and girls in front of her, Miss Mason realized that she faced an enormous task. Perhaps she decided from the beginning to give her very best effort.

Introduction

Establishing missions to educate black boys and girls in a very rural county in the southern part of Alabama area was a very great endeavor. The area is referred to as the Black Belt. The name Black Belt describes the color and richness of the soil which is a strip of land 25-50 miles wide and extends across Alabama and Mississippi.

Six Presbyterian Missions were established in Wilcox County between 1884 and 1903. Three were located on the east side of the Alabama River and three on the west side.

Missions established on the east side of the Alabama River:

Camden Academy	1895
Canton Bend	1896
Miller's Ferry Normal and Industrial School	1884

Missions established on the west side:

Prairie Institute	1894
Midway	1903
Arlington Literary and Industrial High School	1902

Until this period, schools for blacks were few in number and the school term was about three months. The mission school term was eight months. The establishing of schools in an area for blacks where the population consisted of ex-slaves, sharecroppers, servants with excessive poverty and little or no provision for education, such schools can be described as oases for learning. They opened the doors of opportunities for people who had been denied certain rights.

Through the intervention of a Col. William Henderson, a white Presbyterian who came to Alabama after the Civil War, several of the schools were founded. Mr. Henderson became a judge and served the county from 1874-1881.

Administrative History

The United Presbyterian Missions of Wilcox County were established under the auspices of the Freedmen's Board. In late years, the board became The Board of National Mission. Under its leadership was the Women's General Missionary Society (WGMS), which was largely responsible for the financing of the Missions of Wilcox County.

A list of the Board of Directors appears below.

BOARD OF DIRECTORS
WOMEN'S GENERAL MISSIONARY SOCIETY
UNITED PRESBYTERIAN CHURCH OF NORTH AMERICA
1915

Mrs. Mary Clokey Porter, President
Mrs. Samuel Yourd, First Vice President
Miss Jennie H. Clark, Second Vice President
Mrs. John S. Crawford, Recording Secretary
Miss R. Elizabeth Milligan, Literature Secretary
Miss Carrie M. Reed, Editor & Business Manager of Junior Missionary Magazine
Mrs. H. C. Campbell, Foreign Secretary

Mrs. L. H. Milliken, Junior Secretary
Mrs. J. D. Sands, Church Extension and Parsonage
Mrs. Jennie H. Clark, Statistical Secretary
Mrs. R. C. Morton, Temperance Secretary
Mrs. H. Maurice Trimble, Railroad Secretary
Mrs. Mary Clokey Porter, Thank Offering Secretary
Mrs. Ada Kerr Wilson, Indian Secretary & Secretary of Finance
Mrs. J. B. Hill, Ministerial Relief
Mrs. J. B. Hill, Treasurer
Miss Ida B. Little, Young Women's Secretary
Mrs. Samuel Yourd, Freedmen's Secretary

WOMEN'S GENERAL MISSIONARY SOCIETY
UNITED PRESBYTERIAN CHURCH OF NORTH AMERICA
BOARD OF DIRECTORS
1918

Mrs. J. D. Sands, President & Parsonage Secretary
Mrs. William S. Cook, First Vice President & Secretary of Home Mission
Miss Carrie M. Reed, Editor & Business Manager of Junior Missionary Magazine; Treasurer
Mrs. J. B. Hill Treasurer
Mrs. J. Howard Maxwell, Recording Secretary
Mrs. H. C. Campbell, Foreign Secretary
Mrs. Ada Kerr Wilson, Freedmen's Secretary
Mrs. John S. Crawford, Indian Secretary
Mrs. Mary Clokey Porter, Thank Offering Secretary
Miss R. Elizabeth Milligan, Literature Secretary
Mrs. D. James Brown, Statistical Secretary
Miss Ida B. Little, Young Women's Secretary & Secretary of Finance
Mrs. I. H. Milliken, Junior Secretary
Mrs. W. R. Wilson, Railroad Secretary

CHAPTER I

MILLER'S FERRY MISSION
Miller's Ferry, Alabama
Established 1884

Miller's Ferry Mission was the first United Presbyterian Mission School established in Wilcox County for black boys and girls who were descendents of ex-slaves. At the close of the Civil War, a Mr. William Henderson who resided in Ohio moved to Wilcox County and settled in Prairie, Alabama. After settling in Prairie, Mr. Henderson bought large tracts of land and established a farm and a mercantile business. Later, he moved to Miller's Ferry, where he purchased large amounts of land and started the same kinds of businesses. The laborers on his farm were ex-slaves and their offspring. (Johnson, p. 24)

Mr. Henderson, hereafter referred to as Judge Henderson because he became a judge in Wilcox County, was Presbyterian by faith. He became inspired to enlighten his farm workers. Through contacting some of his northern friends and Mrs. Wallace, president of Knoxville College in Knoxville, Tennessee, a school for black students, they succeeded in getting the Freedmen's Board of the United Presbyterian Church to establish a school at Miller's Ferry. Judge Henderson donated 22 ½ acres of land for the site.

In September 1884, a young woman, Miss Henrietta Mason, a graduate of Knoxville College, a United Presbyterian School, was sent to Miller's Ferry to begin the school work. Her classroom was a log church with large holes in its walls. She was the first missionary for the new mission which began with six grades.

After working for three years, Miss Mason was succeeded as principal by Mr. P. C. Cloud in 1887. A three room box schoolhouse was built and the number of teachers increased to three. Later that box schoolhouse building was enlarged to two stories with four classrooms plus a chapel. The number of grades taught increased to eight. Mr. Cloud was the second missionary.

During the early years of the mission, Rev. Charles Henry Johnson, an A. M. E. church pastor in Ohio was asked to come to Miller's Ferry to check on the work there and report his findings. The visit by Rev. Johnson resulted in his becoming principal and pastor of the mission, and the third missionary sent to Miller's Ferry Mission.

Rev. Charles H. Johnson was born in Madison County, West Virginia but his parents moved to Middlesport, Ohio when he was a small boy. He graduated from Knoxville College and completed his theological work at Wilberforce University in Ohio. (Johnson, p. 7)

The fourth missionary sent to Miller's Ferry Normal and Industrial School was Miss Tillie Estelle Glover in 1893. She received her training as a commissioned missionary teacher from Knoxville College. Miss Glover was also a natural musician who could play almost any instrument and sing any vocal part. This natural talent was a great asset in training young people in the work at Miller's Ferry.

In 1894, Rev. Johnson and Miss Tillie Glover were married and continued their work at the mission. (Johnson, p. 31)

THE SCHOOL TRAGEDY

On May 4, 1895, the two-story school building with four rooms and a chapel was destroyed by an incendiary bomb, leaving only the parsonage standing. "On that Sabbath morning there was no bell, no chapel, no pulpit and no Bible from which to read because the building burned on Saturday night." On Sunday morning the

---

Johnson, Sophia Cox, *Beginnings in the Black Belt and Short Stories of the Lives of Dr. Charles Henry and Mrs. Tillie E. Johnson.* 1940, p. 24.

school building and church were smoldering in ashes and coals. The air was filled with sobs and sighs from grown-ups and children, but immediately the people began to improvise a place to hold Sabbath School and worship services." The spot on this Sabbath morning was under an oak tree. (Johnson p. 25)

For several months after the loss of the school building and chapel by fire, some doubt arose as to whether rebuilding would take place to continue the mission work. The Freedmen's Board, however, decided to rebuild and continue its work. The following funds were donated: $500 from the board and $100 from Dr. Witherspoon, Secretary of the Board. The people of the community also made contributions. With these funds in hand, the principal, Rev. Johnson, and community people were anxious to start rebuilding.

Plans for the new building provided for a chapel, 31 x 61, and a wing for two classrooms, 25 x 50. Two classes would be taught in the chapel but there was no provision for four classrooms and four teachers. Dr. C. H. Johnson, principal and pastor of the mission, decided to add another 25 x 50 wing. This brought the total number of classrooms to six.

With the help of the board, Judge Henderson and the people of the community, the new school and chapel were constructed. Now the campus consisted of two buildings, a school building with a chapel and a parsonage. "The task of rebuilding was done by men and women. It is also recorded that women often plowed the fields so the men could work on the new school." The work of the mission continued. (Johnson, Page 23)

THE BEGINNING OF BOARDING DEPARTMENTS

During the early years of the mission school, there was no provision for boarding students. The mission schools and churches were to be community centers. Several changing conditions brought about the idea of boarding departments. The fire had helped to advertise the work of the school and many students were anxious to attend Miller's Ferry Mission School. Because it was a church school, many parents wanted their children to acquire Bible training as well as a secular education.

The question for debate became, what can the school do toward having boarding departments so that boys and girls would not be turned away? Dr. Johnson and the faculty decided to find ways to accommodate boarders. The first step was to organize an industrial class under the direction of vice principal Mr. Green. Step two was to have work periods during which boys chopped and hewed logs. From the logs, a two-room house was built. Work continued until the house would accommodate sixteen boys, yet many boys were turned away. This building was the first boys' dormitory and the third building on the campus.

During the same period, many girls applied for admission to the school. Some provisions had to be made for girls. Again, Judge Henderson came to the rescue and donated all the land needed for the construction of a dorm. At that time, the campus was mostly a thick pine grove, so a site had to be cleaned before construction could begin. A call was made to the men of the community, who were asked to come on a certain night to begin preparing the site. The ladies were asked to bring supper. " That night not over a dozen men responded but equipped with faith, pride, determination and bustle, they set their minds to do the task." (Johnson, p. 27)

Judge Henderson sensed the needs of the builders so he supplied the use of his sawmill, timber, teams, and a sawyer (an individual capable of sawing logs into lumber). A Mr. Thomas Andrews from Allenton, Alabama had a son in the school at the time. Consequently, he had become very interested in the work of the mission. Hearing about the plans to build a girl's dorm, Mr. Andrews came all the way from Allenton to be present on the first night.

All of the things mentioned above proved to be very helpful toward building the dorm, but the school had no money. Exhibiting the same faith used when rebuilding the school, when the school opened the next fall, there was a new girls' dorm with eight rooms, a kitchen and dining room. The dorm accommodated thirty-two girls. The two boys' and girls' dormitories had capacity for forty-eight students. The girls' dorm became the fourth building on the campus. With the addition of two dormitories, the plant now consisted of a school house with chapel, parsonage, teacher's home, a printing and carpenter's shop.

THE HOSPITAL

As part of the curriculum, the school was fortunate to have a hospital to give female students early courses in nurse training. The hospital was founded by Mrs. Tillie Johnson in 1895. Nurses who served the hospital at various times as head nurse throughout the years were Mrs. Nanny Rhea, Mrs. Marzetta Bethea, and Miss Minnie Lee Jones. A doctor from the nearby town of Camden was on call for patients at the hospital.

The hospital was established to serve the communities of Miller's Ferry, Canton Bend, Camden and Prairie. It was named Robinson Memorial.

RETIREMENT OF REV. CHARLES HENRY AND MRS. TILLIE ESTELLE JOHNSON

Rev. and Mrs. Johnson retired from their labor at Miller's Ferry Normal and Industrial School in 1915 and moved to Birmingham, Alabama. Rev. Johnson continued work with the missions in Wilcox County, serving as minister for the Miller's Ferry and Prairie Congregations. He completed forty-two years of service and Mrs. Johnson gave twenty-four years of service. Together they contributed sixty-six years of outstanding work at Prairie and Miller's Ferry.

After moving to Birmingham, Rev. & Mrs. Johnson gave faithful service in Miller Memorial Presbyterian Church, U.S.A. until their passing. They are buried in Grace Hill Cemetery, Birmingham, Alabama.

In chronological order, Rev. I. H. Bonner, a Wilcox County native, succeeded Rev. Johnson as principal and pastor of Miller's Ferry Mission beginning in 1915. During his tenure, the school became a twelfth grade school in 1918 and was renamed Miller's Ferry Normal and Industrial High School. The school continued its rapid growth and its influence was felt far and near. A very important addition was made to the school facilities. The Board of National Missions of the Presbyterian Church constructed a new girl's dorm on the campus.

The dorm was a spacious building consisting of three floors. The first floor, called the basement, consisted of a large dining area where students and teachers ate three meals per day except on Sunday. On Sunday, breakfast and dinner were served, and for supper a brown bag lunch was served. A large kitchen, a laundry and a boiler room were located in the basement. The boiler supplied steam heat for the dorm. The second floor housed a living room, a two-room apartment for the girls' matron, a room for the dietitian, rooms for boarding girls and bath rooms. The dorm had running water, electricity, bathrooms and steam heat.

In 1923, Rev. Charles H. Johnson was invited back to the school by Rev. I. H. Bonner to lay a cornerstone for the new girl's dorm. For that great occasion, Rev. Johnson gave a great inspirational message. His message was as follows:

"Beloved Brethren:

We recognize the goodness of an all wise God, who in the plentitude of his tender mercies and in the wise dispensation of His providential care, has made it possible for us to have this Christian School, and has so adequately provided this additional building for the training of our girls. Therefore we deem it right and appropriate that we do symbolize by some token our lasting gratitude to Him. For that reason we have assembled on this occasion that we might place this stone in the corner of the foundation of this structure.

The Lord say of Himself, 'Behold, I lay in Zion for a foundation a stone, a tried stone, a precious corner stone, a sure foundation. He that believeth shall not make haste.' This stone is but the symbol of that stone which is the living Christ, who is the inspiration and the strength on whom we must depend. They that trust in the Lord shall be as Mount Zion which cannot be removed. This building consecrated, as it is to a holy purpose that of Christian training is but the emblem in its work of that nobler building the spiritual house of God, of which the apostle says Christ Himself is the Chief Corner Stone.

It is right and proper that we publicly acknowledge our dependence upon God, both in an effort to erect a house for Christian service and this stone represents a great sentiment and keeps before us a fundamental truth, 'Except the Lord builds the house, they labor in vain that build it.'

We are reminded that it is not in ourselves but in Him that we overcome. In the name of Him and His service, we place this stone in its place, indicating the connecting point, the firmness and completeness of the whole foundation emblematic of the great spiritual temple to which it points." (Johnson, pp. 28-29)

Rev. I. H. Bonner left the institution in 1921 and joined the ministry of the African Methodist Episcopal Church, where he became a bishop. Professor C. S. Simpson, a graduate of Knoxville College, became the new principal.

Several important improvements were made under Professor Simpson's leadership. The Wilcox County Board of Education erected a new high school building. At the outset the building did not have a gymnasium. A gym was added in later years.

On May 13, 1930, the Wilcox County Board of Education accepted bids for the construction of two school buildings.

An Excerpt from the Board of Education

Board of Education:

"It is hereby ordered that the contract for the construction of the Snow Hill Institute building for Negroes at Snow Hill be awarded to F. D. Kimbrough, Pine Hill, Alabama, at $31,833.00 and the contract for the construction of the county training school for Negroes at Miller's Ferry be awarded to Aiken and Faulkner, Atlanta, Georgia, at $9,822.30. W. J. Jones, Superintendent, as Executive Officer of the Wilcox County Board of Education, is hereby authorized to sign the contract for the construction of the Snow Hill building as soon as $10,000.00 of the $25,000.00 General Education Board's appropriation for this project is deposited with the Wilcox County Treasurer of School Funds by the General Education board and an agreement reached with the General Education as to the manner of their depositing the remainder of their appropriation for this building, and to sign the contract for the construction of the Miller's Ferry School building immediately upon deposit with the Wilcox County Treasurer of School Funds of $5,122.30 by the Miller's Ferry School. Further order is that an additional state aid appropriation of $900.00 be allowed the Miller's Ferry project, making a total of $2,700.00 state aid for Miller's Ferry and $2,100.00 state aid for Snow Hill Institute."

After the new school building was constructed, Miller's Ferry Normal and Industrial High School was renamed Wilcox County Training School. The County Board had become involved with a mission school for the first time. Some teachers began receiving their salaries from the Wilcox County Board of Education. The Presbyterian Board continued to operate the school as it had in the previous years by paying some teachers and maintaining the physical plant. Bible study was continued. The first high school class to graduate under the new name Wilcox County Training School was in 1930.

In the early thirties, the County Board also constructed a vocational building at Miller's Ferry under the Smith Hughes Act. Home Economics and Vocational Agriculture now became an integral part of the school's curriculum.

The thirties were the Depression years, yet the missions vigorously pursued their goals of helping students to obtain an education. The boarding departments continued to be a vital part of the work. Students, both boys and girls, from Chicago, Birmingham, Selma and Mobile continued to come as boarding students, while students also came from the rural areas in Wilcox, Monroe, Clark, Marengo, Dallas, Choctaw and Jefferson Counties.

Professor C. S. Simpson passed away in 1936 while still serving as principal. He was carried back to his home in Tennessee and buried there.

Following the demise of Professor Simpson, Professor Norman D. Williams became principal of Wilcox

County Training School in 1936. Up to that time, Professor Williams and his family resided at Annemanie, Alabama, where he was employed as a teacher.

Under the leadership of Professor Williams, other important improvements were made. A school bus was purchased by Professor Williams so more students could be transported to high school from the communities of Flatwood, Catherine, Gastonburg, Prairie and Midway. The bus was blue and white in color, so students named it "The Blue Goose." Before the bus was provided, some students walked a round trip of twelve miles daily in order to attend high school. Professor Williams was instrumental in getting a program under which high school students could work and earn money in order to pay their room and board. This program was the N. Y. A., The National Youth Administration.

With the help of the N. Y. A. program, several new buildings were constructed. These were a teacher's home, a new boys' dormitory replacing the earlier dorm which was destroyed by fire, and a tin shop which housed a canning plant. A new elementary building was started by the N. Y. A. Program which was discontinued before the building was completed. The Women's General Missionary Society under the National Board of Missions took over the task of completing the elementary building and financed it to completion in 1944. The National Youth Administration was founded in 1935 to provide job training for unemployed youths and part-time work for needy students.

The canning factory was very helpful for a period of time. Farmers from various communities brought farm animals, vegetables and fruits to be canned. The project was helpful to the farm families and to the school because farmers paid for the service by giving the school a certain percentage of the canned products.

THE YELLOW SCHOOL BUSES

In 1953, the Wilcox County Board of Education provided two new yellow school buses to transport students to the County Training school using the previously established route used by "The Blue Goose."

After the death of Professor Williams in 1951, the reins of the school were taken over by Professor Booker T. Ridgeway. The only remaining workers at the school who were paid by the Presbyterian Board were two lunchroom workers, a dormitory matron and a Bible teacher. The girl's dorm was destroyed by fire in 1963 and was not rebuilt. A much smaller block building was constructed which housed the lunchroom and a few rooms to accommodate a small number of girl borders and female teachers.

At a particular time during its long history, Miller's Ferry campus had the following buildings.

1. A principal's home
2. A chapel (school combined)
3. A gymnasium
4. Vocational building
5. A cannery
6. Three cottages for teacher families
7. A garage, N. Y. A. barracks, and a tog house
8. A school building for high school students
9. A band room
10. An elementary building
11. Girls' dorm
12. Boys' dorm
13. Parsonage

After the passage of the Civil Rights Act of 1965, more changes occurred at Wilcox County Training School. A Bible teacher was no longer employed and the principal, B. T. Ridgeway, was able to persuade the Board of National Missions to pay for a kindergarten teacher. The board agreed and a kindergarten program was initiated.

Professor Ridgeway retired in 1972, the same year that the National Board completely severed its relationship with the mission schools.

Professor and Mrs. Laura Ridgeway retired to Selma, Alabama, where he passed away in 1973.

The school was no longer a mission school. It was completely under the auspices of the Wilcox County Board of Education. It remained a high school under the principalship of Mr. B. T. Hollinger for one year.

In 1973, the high school department at Wilcox County Training School was discontinued and the high school students were transported by bus to Camden Academy. The elementary department, kindergarten through sixth grade, was continued until 1979.

In the fall of that year, the elementary school was discontinued. Students on the west side of the Alabama River were sent to Alberta Elementary School and students on the east side were sent to Camden Academy. This action completely marked the end of a school era at Miller's Ferry, Alabama.

Principal and minister of Miller's Ferry Normal and Industrial School
later named Wilcox County Training School:

Rev. Charles H. Johnson
Rev. I. H. Bonner
Professor C. S. Simpson
Professor Norman D. Williams
Professor B. T. Ridgeway
Professor B. T. Hollinger

Other ministers who served:

Rev. D. F. White
Rev. James F. Reese
Rev. Thomas L. Threadgill

Persons who served as elementary principals after the close of the high school were Rev. Eades Primm, Mrs. Jeannette S. McCall and Mrs. Mildred Connie J. Patterson Sanders.

The United Presbyterian Church of North America was involved with the Miller's Ferry Mission for eighty-seven years. It must be noted that for the majority of these years, the Church never faltered in its endeavor for it continued providing facilities, maintenance and putting money directly into the budget of the Wilcox County Board of Education.

Peter C. Cloud
Teacher at Miller's Ferry

Reverend Charles Henry Johnson, D. D.
Principal/Pastor of Miller's Ferry Mission
After his retirement in 1915 he served as pastor of Prairie Presbyterian
Church as well as the Miller's Ferry Presbyterian Church

Mrs. Tillie Johnson
A teacher at Miller's Ferry Normal and Industrial School
for 24 years

Rev. I. H. Bonner
Principal & Pastor
Miller's Ferry Normal & Industrial High School
Pastor at Prairie

Professor Curtis S. Simpson
Principal of Miller's Ferry Normal and
Industrial High School

COMPLIMENTS OF THE CLASS OF

1927

The Senior Class
of
Nineteen Hundred and
Twenty-Seven
Miller's Ferry
Normal School
announces its
Commencement Exercises
Wednesday Afternoon,
May eleventh,
at 2:30 o'clock
Miller's Ferry Chapel

Gideon Beck
John Bethea,
Early Camel,
Marie Carter,
Estella Culpepper,
Ethel England,
James Fisher,
Katie M. Godfery,
Olivia Harris,
Ethel M. Jones,
Bennie McArthur,
Lonnie Norwood,
Annie K. Parker,
Minnie Steele,
Eudora Sykes,
Daisy Smith,
Theodore Smith

Motto: "The Ladder of Success is Now Before us."

Class Flower: White Rose.

Class Colors:
Emeral Green & Old Gold

Class
of
1927

GRADUATION EXERCISES

Miller's Ferry Chapel

Wednesday, May 11th, 2:30 p.m.

Processional

Music.........Female Quartet

Invocation

Music..........Male Quartet

Oration........"Negro In Music"
Eudora Sykes

Music.........Instrumental Solo
Eudora Sykes

Oration...."Negro In Literature"
Annie K. Parker

Music.........Female Quartet

Address........Dr. P. W. Walls
Birmingham, AL

Music

Presentation of Diplomas

Announcements

Benediction

1927

The original Miller's Ferry Chapel as it looked in the year 2001
Its use as a church was discontinued in 1971.

Professor Norman D. Williams
Principal
Wilcox County Training School at Miller's Ferry 1936-1951

Boy's Dorm at Miller's Ferry
This building was destroyed by fire.

Girls' Dorm
Dedicated in 1923 by Rev. Charles H. Johnson
This building was destroyed by fire in 1963.

Professor and Mrs. B. T. Ridgeway
Served as teachers 1929 – 1951
Professor Ridgeway served as Principal, Wilcox County Training School
1951 – 1972

Wilcox County Training High School Building
Constructed in 1930 by the Wilcox County Board of Education

Miller's Ferry Hospital
Robinson Memorial

13

1972 CANDIDATES FOR GRADUATION

Anderson, Frank
Bates, Geraldine M.
Brown, Donald J.
Burwell, Shirley
Coleman, Annie B.
Cox, Thelma M.
Crear, Barbara D.
Harris, Robert
Johnson, Curtis
Jones, Juanita
Latham, Verna
Lawson, Bernice I.
Mack, Barbara A.
McCall, Kenneth

Miller, Jeremiah
Mixon, Charles
Mixon, Ralph **
Pettway, Marva
Pettway, Ruth
Robinson, Aaron
Robinson, Polly
Robinson, Richard
Ross, Arthur
Scott, Roberta D. ***
Smith, Inell
Thurman, Luellen *
Williams, Carolyn

*** 1st Honor
** 2nd Honor
* 3rd Honor

CLASS COLORS
Blue and White

CLASS FLOWER
Blue Carnation

CLASS MOTTO
"I will study and prepare myself, and when opportunity presents itself, I will be ready."

The Eighty-Eighth

Annual Commencement

OF THE

Wilcox County Training School

THE SCHOOL AUDITORIUM

Thursday, May 25, 1972
1:00 P.M.
Miller's Ferry, Alabama

PROGRAM

*PROCESSIONAL — War March of the Priests from *"Athalia"*
by Mendelssohn-E. Pauer

*INVOCATION

MUSIC .... *"Softly as the Light of Morning"* .... Ira B. Wilson

ORATION .... *"Staking our Claim"* .... Ralph Mixon

ORATION .... *"Not the End, the Beginning"* .... Roberta Diana Scott

MUSIC .... *"Holy, Holy, Holy"* .... Franz Schubert

PRESENTATION OF GUEST SPEAKER .... Mr. B. T. Ridgeway

ADDRESS .... Rev. C. C. Brown
Pastor, Reformed Presbyterian Church
Selma, Alabama

MUSIC .... *"Give me your tired, your poor"* ...... arr. Roy Ringwald

PRESENTATION OF CANDIDATES FOR DIPLOMAS

REMARKS AND ANNOUNCEMENTS

*SCHOOL SONG

*BENEDICTION

*RECESSIONAL .... *"Pomp and Circumstance"* .... Elgar

Dear Ole Alma Mater,
Stand forever loyal.
Keep forever going high
Our beams of deity.
Guide us ever onward;
Keep our spirits loyal
Help us fight for truth and right
For ole M. F. High.

*Congregation please stand

The Last High School Commencement Program held on the same campus
where Miller's Ferry Normal and Industrial High School began.

CHAPTER II

PRAIRIE INSTITUTE
Prairie, Alabama
Established 1894

After the Presbyterian School was established at Miller's Ferry, it is believed that Judge Henderson was largely responsible for Prairie's decision to petition the same board for a Christian school at Prairie. A petition was sent by a group of Prairie people to the Freedmen's Board of the United Presbyterian Church to start a mission in Prairie. The request was granted and the judge donated the land on which the small church that he built earlier stood for a school. The Baptist and Methodist congregations were already established in the community so each used the same small church on a designated Sunday.

The Women's Missionary Society under the Freedmen's Board was put in charge and work on the school began immediately. In 1895, the new school building was completed and was named in honor of Mrs. Jennie Hastings Gillespie, the first secretary of the societies. A plaque on the wall in the building serves as a cornerstone. A piano was also donated in her honor. The piano remains in the school chapel. Although in poor condition, a tune of sorts can still be played on it.

THE SCHOOL BUILDING

The School building was constructed by Rev. J. T. Arter, who served as principal and farm manager from 1894 to 1900 at Prairie.

The building as it was originally built consisted of six available classrooms. A very large room in the center of the building was divided by large panels, which could be separated to make one large room into two classrooms. For daily chapel exercise, the panels were pushed back to form a large room to accommodate grades one through nine. The building is made of wood and is well kept. There is a steeple and a bell atop the building. Seeing the school for the first time, one may readily think that it is a church. Many visitors do think so even to the present. When the school building was first erected, it was said to be the finest school for blacks in Wilcox County.

In 1900, Rev. J. T. Arter was transferred to Annemanie, Alabama to establish a mission school there. Mr. N. B. Cotton, a Knoxville College graduate, became director of the farm and Rev. J. E. James assumed the role of pastor and principal.

THE SCHOOL FARM

In 1896, the Women's Board purchased 626 acres of land from Judge Henderson. The land was to be subdivided into plots of forty acres more or less and sold to tenants living on the land. This plan wasn't very successful because only one local family purchased fifty acres of that land, which remains in possession of that particular family. In 1929, the remaining land was resold to the sons of Judge Henderson, and about sixty acres were retained for the school.

Four men served as property managers. They were Rev. J. H. Oliver, Professor N. B. Cotton, Mr. I. L. Dumas and Mr. Fred Bennett.

THE CHURCH

Prairie has its own small white church with ax-hewn sills. At the beginning, the church was located on the same side of the road as the school building. In 1937, under the auspices of Professor Peters, the church building was torn down and then constructed on the opposite side of the road where it still stands today.

THE CAMPUS LAYOUT

It is not possible to give the chronological order for the construction of various buildings, but at one time the campus consisted of the following buildings: a school, church, teachers' home, parsonage, girls' and boys' dormitories and a shop. In later years, the teachers' home was used only by the principal and his family. The girls' dorm was named Yourd Hall in honor of Mrs. Yourd, who at the time it was constructed served as secretary for mission work in Wilcox County for the United Presbyterian Church.

When Prairie Institute was established, the buildings were located on both sides of the County road, which ran to Prairie Bluff and the Alabama River. On the south side of the road, the school building, church and boys' dorm and the shop were situated, while on the north side of the road, a parsonage, a girls' dorm and the teachers' home were located. Today, the school, church and teacher's home are the only remaining buildings.

THE STUDENT BODY

The student body was made up of students from the surrounding communities and counties of Marengo and Dallas. Some students boarded with relatives in the community near the school, while others came and lived in the boarding departments by paying for their lodging. Many students walked long distances daily to attend school.

A school record shows that in 1914-1915 about 131 students were enrolled in grades 1-9. After graduating from Prairie Institute, many students continued their education at Miller's Ferry Normal and Industrial School after it became a high school in 1918. Some students lived in the dormitories and a few commuted by car, crossing the Alabama River on a ferry. When the river overflowed its bank during the school year, students rode across floodwater in a skiff.

SCHOOL LIFE AT PRAIRIE

The school day began at 8:00 each morning five days per week and closed at 3:00 in the afternoon with a half-hour for recess at noon. School began early September and ran until early May. Homework was assigned and students were expected to prepare this work before coming to school.

The school bell played an important part during the school day. The first bell sounded at 7:00, the second bell at 7:45 and the third bell rang at 8:00. By this time, students were required to be in their classrooms.

EXTRA CURRICULAR ACTIVITIES

All students were required to learn academics and Bible but there were extra curricular activities as well. A literary club met each Friday afternoon at the last class period. Students took part by singing, reciting poetry, reciting famous quotations, and holding debates. Other special activities were programs for holidays, Bible contests, concerts by classes and Commencement Exercises.

The Bible contest was not compulsory, but to participate a student was required to memorize a chapter of scripture. Then on a given occasion, students would compete against each other by reciting different Bible chapters. There were judges and three prizes were awarded. The first prize was $1.00, the second $.75 and the third was $.50. Big money!

The Mother's Club

Prairie Institute prided itself on having an excellent Mother's Club consisting of the women of the community. This club was helpful to the school and community because the club sponsored an annual picnic for teachers and students, gave an annual concert and an exhibit of their sewing, speaking, singing and arts. This club could be considered a forerunner of today's P. T. O. because parents were instructed on ways to help children become better students.

The Bells

Prairie Institute was also the recipient of two excellent bells which were shipped to Prairie from Pennsylvania. One hangs in the steeple of the school building and the other one in the steeple of the church. These bells were an integral part of the school and church life. Five days per week, the school bell was rung to bring the student body together. On Sunday mornings the church bell was rung as a reminder of Sabbath School and Church. Bells are built with a specific tone. The school bell has a "C" tone and the church bell has an "E" tone.

For many years, the bells were sounded to remind the community of two other very significant events. On the last night in December, the young men and teenage boys rang the bells for at least half an hour beginning before midnight and continued into the New Year for at least the same amount of time. This practice was called 'ringing out the old year and ringing in the New Year." These bell ringers were very enthusiastic about this practice and continued it for many, many years. For miles around, people listened to hear these bells on New Year's night.

A second significant practice was tolling of the bell. This signified to the community that someone had passed. Night or day, the bell was tolled when a death occurred.

In the spring of the year, there was a clean-up day. Students and teachers worked very diligently to spruce up the campus. Grounds were cleaned, flowers and trees were planted. Rocks and tree trunks were whitewashed for a fresh look.

Commencement Exercises

Commencement Exercises climaxed the school year. The day before, the building was cleaned by students until it was spick-and-span. The special program consisted of Valedictorian and Salutatorian speakers, special music, plus an out of town guest speaker. Commencement day was an exciting time for parents, students and teachers, friends and former graduates. The class speakers memorized their orations. There was no reading of these speeches.

We also think it would be well to mention by name some of the very, very early teachers who served at Prairie and did remarkable work. The names honor many men and women: Mr. L. W. Michael, Misses Totten, Upton and Bradford, Mr. Sally, Professor Cary, Mr. A. H. Adams, Mrs. Stevens, Mrs. Elliot, Mrs. Tillie Johnson and Mr. Homer Fowler. Among the white friends who befriended the school were the Wiltsies, the Bruce Brothers, the Arringtons, Hendersons, and Dr. Pernell.

When the county schools were mandated to integrate, Prairie Institute was under the auspices of the Wilcox County Board of Education for about fourteen years. However, the Mission Board continued to pay a Bible teacher, a maintenance worker, and maintained the buildings and grounds.

Around 1968, the school was consolidated with Wilcox County Training School. It had served Prairie and surrounding areas for seventy-seven years.

Prairie Mission (Prairie Institute) was served by an excellent group of principals and ministers, some of whom served a double role:

Rev. J. T. Arter -	Principal/Pastor
	Prairie's First Principal 1894-1900
Rev. James -	Principal/Pastor 1900 -
Rev. Imes -	Principal/Pastor buried in the church cemetery at Prairie
	One of his two sons served as president of Knoxville College
Rev. J. N. Cotton -	Later moved to serve Canton Bend Mission
Professor James -	Principal
Professor T. M. Elliot -	Principal
Rev. J. E. Wade -	Principal/Pastor 1921-1929
Professor William T. Peters -	Principal 1929-1957
	Served the longest term, 28 years
Professor Palmer E. Williams -	Principal 1957-1968

Other ministers who served the Prairie Congregation were:

Rev. D. F. White
Rev. Charles H. Johnson
Rev. Richard P. Williams
Rev. Claude C. Brown
Rev. Benjamin F. Thompson
Rev. I. H. Bonner

Professor J. T. Arter
Principal – Prairie Institute 1894 – 1900
Arlington Literary and Industrial High School 1900 – 1918
First Principal of Prairie Institute

SALE OF LAND LETTERS

On the following pages two letters show the transaction of fifty acres of land sold to Mr. and Mrs. Noy Steele of Prairie, Alabama. This is the only family who purchased land. The land still remains in the family.

Women's General Missionary Society
United Presbyterian Church of North America
Board of Directors

Foreign Secretary
Mrs. H. C. Campbell
340 S. Hiland Ave., Pittsburgh, Pa.

Freedmen's Secretary
Mrs. Ada Kerr Wilson
1112 South Ave., Wilkinsburg, Pa.

Indian Secretary
Mrs. John S. Crawford
95 Trenton Ave., Wilkinsburg, Pa.

Thank Offering Secretary
Mrs. Mary Clokey Porter
2828 Perrysville Ave.,
N. S., Pittsburgh, Pa.

Literature Secretary
Miss R. Elizabeth Milligan
5534 Kentucky Ave., Pittsburgh, Pa.

**President and
Parsonage Secretary**
Mrs. J. D. Sands
137 Roup St., Pittsburgh, Pa.

**First Vice President and
Secretary of Home Missions**
Mrs. Wm. S. Cook
1201 6th Ave., Beaver Falls, Pa.

**Second Vice President
Editor and Business Manager of
Junior Missionary Magazine**
Miss Carrie M. Reed
406 S. Evaline St., Pittsburgh, Pa.

Treasurer
Mrs. J. B. Hill
5845 Marlborough St.
Pittsburgh, Pa.

Recording Secretary
Mrs. J. Howard Maxwell
142 Taylor Ave.,
Beaver, Pa.

Statistical Secretary
Mrs. D. James Brown
15 N. Fremont Ave., Bellevue, Pa.

**Young Women's Secretary
and Secretary of Finance**
Miss Ida B. Little
132 Allison Ave., Washington, Pa.

Junior Secretary
Mrs. I. H. Milliken
205 Lexington Ave., Aspinwall,
Pittsburgh, Pa.

Temperance Secretary

Railroad Secretary
Mrs. W. R. Wilson
328 Dalzell Ave., Ben Avon, Pa.

November 6, 1918

Mr. Noy Steel.

Dear Mr. Steel:—

I presented your request to buy 25 more acres of Prairie land to the Board at its meeting yesterday and hasten to inform you of the action taken because I know you are anxious to hear the decision.

The Board is favorable to the request, but wishes me to take up the matter of the location of the land together with the price, with a Committee composed of Judge Henderson, Rev. Johnson & Mr. Dumas — I will write to them immediately & when I receive their opinion. I will again write to you, telling you the final decision both as to location & price. I am sure we will be glad to have you stay on the farm.

Very truly yours,

Carnegie Pa Feb. 3rd 1915—

Dear Mr Steel;—

Our Attorney has prepared a Deed for the plot land you wish to buy. It is now in the hands of the officers of the Board to be signed by them & witnessed by a "Notary Public" And will probably be in Mr Dumas hands before March 1st. Please read the paper carefully And be sure you note the clause which reads that in case you wish to sell, the Board's consent must be obtained. That gives us the chance to buy it back in case an undesirable purchaser might appear And is only meant to safe guard the school. However we want you to be sure you understand this And hence you had better file this letter with your deed when you get it. Be sure & have the Deed recorded in your County court records. Our Attorney says the forms of mortgage used in the various States are so different that you had better have one drawn up in your own State. The deed says you are to pay one hundred dollars on delivery of the deed And the balance two hundred & seventy five ($275) in four years with interest at 4%. Payment on said mortgage

Prairie Institute School Building

Prairie Presbyterian Church
Rebuilt in 1937 by Mr. Otto Haynes, Mr. Wilmer and Mr. Danny Bridges

Prof. T. M. Elliot
Principal – Prairie Institute

Professor and Mrs. J. E. Wade
Prairie Institute Mission School

Prof. William T. Peters
Principal of Prairie Institute School

A Prairie Institute School Faculty
Left to right: Prof. Peters, Mrs. Estella Perkins, Mrs. Hope Edwards,
Mrs. Etoile Peters, Mrs. Fannie Ross Bennett and Mr. James Rivers
Year 1930

Mr. Isaac F. Dumas
Farm manager at Prairie Institute
Ministers at Prairie Presbyterian Church

Mrs. Isaac L. Dumas
A teacher at Prairie Institute
and Arlington Literary and
Industrial School

Dr. Claude C. Brown
Served as minister for Arlington and Prairie Congregations
1945 – 1963

Rev. Benjamin F. Thompson
Served Prairie Presbyterian and Arlington Presbyterian Church
1963 - 1992

Bells at Prairie Institute
The bells were shipped from Pennsylvania to Prairie, Alabama

1914–15. NAMES. Fourth Grade	M.	T.	W.	T.	F.	M.	T.	W.	T.	F.	M.	T.	W.	T.	F.	M.	T.	W.	T.	F.	M. SUM.	M.	T.	W.	T.	F.
September																										
1. Bennett Loetta		4																								
2. Eaton Janie L.		5																								
3. Gaston Mary		4																								
4. Gradford Mattie		5																								
5. Harris Nancy		5																								
6. Hudson Maggie		5																								
7. Pernell Virginia		5																								
8. Molden Lizzie		5																								
9. Smith Roberta																										
10. Vaughn Wiltzie L.																										
11. Marsh Pinkie																										
12. Sykes Emmeline																										
Third Grade																										
1. Flemming Ralph	4																									
2. Foster Lidell	X																									
3. Green Carl	4																									
4. Miller Henry	X																									
5. Smith Elmore	4																									
6. Stowe Reynolds	X																									
7. Shores Robert Lee																										
8. Terry Willie	4																									
9. Tripp Tommy																										
1. Ikleheimer Lexanna	4																									
2. Johnson Georgia	4																									
3. Steele Florence	4																									

School Record from Prairie Institute

This is to certify that

Prairie Mission

which has been selected as a landmark contributing to a
deeper understanding of our American Heritage

has been entered on

The National Register of Historic Places

by the

United States Department of the Interior

October 29, 2001
Date Entered

_____
Governor, State of Alabama

_____
Chairman

Alabama Historical Commission

_____
Secretary of State

_____
Executive Director

The Alabama Register of Historic Places and the National Register of Historic Places

26

CHAPTER III

CAMDEN ACADEMY
Camden, Alabama
Established 1895

In 1895, Camden Academy was the third mission school established under the auspices of the United Presbyterian Church of North America in Wilcox County. The site chosen for this school was atop a hill just outside the town limits of Camden, the county seat. The hill was known as Hangman's Hill.

The campus consisted of two small, one-room buildings and began with grades 1-8. As the school grew, other buildings were added. The school's first principal was Mr. Henry Green, who served from 1895-1897. The next principal was Rev. R. K. Smith, who served as principal and minister from 1897-1905. During his tenure, the physical plant was enlarged. A combination chapel and school, two dormitories for boarding students, one for girls and one for boys, and a teachers' home were added.

In 1905, Rev. and Mrs. W. G. Wilson came to Camden Academy as the new missionaries. Rev. Wilson was a graduate of Temple University in Pennsylvania. He served as minister and principal.

As an excellent educator, Rev. Wilson was able to make great progress in the school's academic program. Under his guidance, the school became a high school. The first high school class graduated from the institution in 1930. Three mission schools in Wilcox County now provided high school training for black boys and girls: Miller's Ferry Normal and Industrial High School, Camden Academy and Arlington Literary and Industrial High School. Until this period Snow Hill Institute was the only other high school in Wilcox County for black pupils.

In 1910-1911, Rev. Wilson interrupted his tenure as principal of Camden Academy by spending a year at Miller Memorial Presbyterian in Birmingham, Alabama; however, he returned to Camden Academy the following year, where he remained until his death.

While holding the reins as principal, Rev. Wilson taught math classes. As a writer, he wrote poetry of great significance. The school had a well-trained band which performed concerts at various places in the county as well as at home. Rev. Wilson passed away in 1935, and was buried on the school campus where he served for thirty-four years.

The year was 1935. One of Camden academy's graduates came home to take charge of the high school from which he had graduated. This individual was Professor Alfonso Peoples. Professor Peoples and his wife, Mrs. Gladys Peoples, were well trained and very energetic, so they immediately began making necessary improvements in order to take the school to new heights.

One of the first improvements was to upgrade the faculty by hiring teachers with degrees from various colleges. The size of the physical plant needed to be increased to provide for growth. To accomplish the expansion, the girls' dormitory at Prairie Institute, Yourd Hall, which was no longer needed to accommodate boarders, was torn down and the building materials were transported to Camden to help in the construction plan. A principal's home and expanded quarters for teachers and an Industrial Arts Building were added.

Under the administration of Professor Peoples, the school, with its large enrollment of transported and boarding students, improved curriculum and higher educational standards, and a highly trained faculty was rewarded by becoming Wilcox County's first Black accredited High School. A couple of other very significant changes occurred during this period. The Wilcox County Public School System was now transporting students from several communities to Camden Academy. The boys and girls dorms were no longer as necessary as they were many years earlier. In the forties, during Professor Peoples' tenure all faculty except the Bible teacher, maintenance worker, janitor and the dietitian were paid by the county. However, by the late forties and early fifties all teachers were paid by the county. Bible teachers, sewing teachers and janitors were still paid by the Board of National Missions.

In 1960, Professor Peoples resigned as principal and he and Mrs. Peoples moved to Chattanooga, Tennessee. He became principal of a high school in Chattanooga.

Many changes had come about at Camden Academy but the school continued to do and emphasize many of the things that were done as a mission school. The student body and faculty continued those exemplary qualities for which the school was noted.

CAMDEN ACADEMY AND THE CIVIL RIGHTS YEARS

In 1960 Professor and Mrs. James Hobbs came to Camden Academy. Professor Hobbs was the new principal and the civil rights movement was beginning to take shape. Many students and teachers became involved in the movement.

The period from 1965-1974 can be described as years of great struggle and involvement in civil rights for students, teachers and parents of Camden Academy. The whole school system was involved because Wilcox County was mandated to integrate its public schools. Many students and teachers became very active in the struggle for equal educational opportunities and voting rights.

Camden Academy was located within close proximity of the business section of the town of Camden. This may have proved helpful to the many individuals who demonstrated their beliefs against segregation.

What transpired at Camden Academy next is described in the minutes of the Wilcox County Board of Education dated August 17, 1965. The board passed the following resolution:

WHEREAS, the Wilcox County Board of Education has the power, and the duty of, and is vested with, the general administration and supervision of the public schools and educational interests of Wilcox County, Alabama, and is responsible for and has the duty of operating free public school with Wilcox County, Alabama, and

WHEREAS, The Board of National Missions and the United Presbyterian Church in the United States of America, a Corporation, owns 29.3 acres of land and described in that certain deed recorded in Book DD, page 33, Probate Office of Wilcox County, Alabama less and except 8 acres thereof deeded the State of Alabama by deeds recorded in Deed Book 4-M, page 414 and Deed Book 5-S, page 371, Probate Office of Wilcox County, Alabama; said property aforesaid owned by Board of National Missions of the United Presbyterian Church in the United States of America, A Corporation, being operated and known as Camden Academy; and

WHEREAS, on the property aforesaid there are buildings that are used for school purposes and that are not used for school purposes; and, on the property aforesaid of the State of Alabama and Wilcox County Board of Education two school buildings that are now used for classroom teaching; and

WHEREAS, the Wilcox County Board of Education is contemplating additional construction of school building necessary to accommodate the education of Wilcox County youth; and to facilitate additional construction necessary at the location known as Camden Academy there is a needed additional land; and, if necessary to the administration and supervision of the public schools and educational interests of Wilcox County, Alabama, that the land and buildings thereon at the location known as Camden Academy, Wilcox County, Alabama, now owned by the Board of National Missions of the United Presbyterian Church in the United States of America, a Corporation, be acquired by the Wilcox County Board of Education, and that such would be in the public interest and necessary for public school purposes; Now there,

BE IT RESOLVED by the WILCOX COUNTY BOARD OF EDUCATION that the property now owned by the Board of National Missions of the United Presbyterian Church in the United States of America, a Corporation, at its location known as Camden Academy, Camden,

Alabama, more particularly described in Exhibit "A": attached hereto, be acquired in the fee simple title by the exercise of eminent domain right of the Wilcox County Board of Education for public use of school purposes.

In the above transaction, the Wilcox County Board of Education paid the Board of National Missions, $40,000.00 for the property.

In 1952, a separate church building was erected on the campus. The Rev. James F. Reese was its first minister. After the school and property were taken over in 1965 by the County School Board, the original school was condemned and torn down. The church building, constructed in 1952, was also torn down because it could not remain on the county premises.

From the year 1895 to 1972, the United Presbyterian Church of North America was involved in the work with Camden Academy.

The school population of Camden Academy increased in the school year 1973-1974 when Wilcox County Training School was discontinued and the high school students were bussed to Camden Academy which is now a County Board of Education School. In 1974, the last high school class was graduated under the original name Camden Academy. Camden Academy became a middle school and grades 9-12 were transferred to Wilcox County High School on Broad Street in Camden.

After 1974, Camden Academy became an elementary and a middle school with a separation of grades K-4 and 5-8 in different buildings with separate principals. Professor Hobbs was named principal of grades K-4 and Professor Zack Z. Brown became principal of grades 5-8. The elementary school K-4 was named J. E. Hobbs Elementary.

Looking back at the years, the resources and energy which were used to make this school into the great institution which it became can be judged by its successful students and those who are still committed to its ideals. It is quite fitting to present an Honor Roll of those who served in the role of principal and pastor. No attempt will be made to enumerate teachers and others because the list would be too long to remember all of these dedicated workers. It can be said that teachers who served in the mission schools came from various states and many parts of Alabama. Some of the states were Ohio, Mississippi, Tennessee, Kentucky, Virginia and Pennsylvania.

The last class graduated under the name Camden Academy in 1974. Hence, we think it is justifiable to say that the school's seventy-nine year legacy on top of Hangman's Hill can be referred to as "Remarkable Years" in the history of education for black boys and girls.

Principals/Ministers who served Camden Academy
Prof. Henry Green	1895-1897
Rev. R. K. Smith	1897-1905
Rev. W. G. Wilson	1905-1935
Prof. Alfonso Peoples	1935-1960
Prof. James Hobbs	1960-1974

Other Ministers who served were:
Rev. D. F. White
Rev. James F. Reese
Rev. Thomas L. Threadgill

The Camden Academy School Building

Mr. William G. Wilson
1911 - 1935

Mr. Alphonso Curtis Peoples
1935 - 1960

Professor. E. Hobbs
Camden Academy 1960 – 1974

Rev. & Mrs. D. F. White
Pastored Prairie, Midway, Camden, Canton Bend and Miller's Ferry
during his years of service as a minister in Wilcox County

Rev. James Foster Reese
Pastor – Trinity Presbyterian Church
Camden, Alabama 1952 - 1958

Rev. Thomas L. Threadgill
Pastor – Trinity Presbyterian Church
Camden, Alabama 1971 - 1989

Our Pastor and Chapel

We look about us to find that our main purpose for being here is to live. I dare you to think of another reason. But there is a great and present danger that we forget that ONLY reason. We ask, then, the same as a sage of our own generation: "What happened to the life we have lost in living? What has happened to the wisdom we have lost in knowledge?" That main reason is still to live, but we still neglect to do it. Let us cease living for that which is not life.

T. L. Threadgill
Died 1989

CHAPTER IV

CANTON BEND MISSION

In 1896, still another mission under the Board of National Missions was founded in Wilcox County at Canton Bend. Canton Bend is approximately eleven miles west of Camden. The school consisted of grades 1-8. Rev. N. B. Cotton, who had earlier served Prairie Institute as pastor and principal, was put in charge of the new mission. The mission consisted of an academic building with a chapel, a parsonage and a teacher's home. This was the fourth mission and it was modeled after the earlier ones already established in the county.

After his years of service, Rev. Cotton retired and returned to his native home in North Carolina. The school and church continued to serve the community under the leadership of Mr. Theodore R. Kimmons and Mr. Lawrence Parrish. After the retirement of Rev. Cotton, Rev. D. F. White and Rev. James F. Reese at different intervals served as ministers.

During the fifties, the academic building and chapel were destroyed by fire. The students from Canton Bend were bused to Camden Academy. This marked the end of the era for Canton Bend. Without exception, there were hundreds of individuals who referred to this school as their Alma Mater.

Rev. N. B. Cotton
Principal and Pastor of Canton Bend United Presbyterian Mission

Chapter V

Arlington Literary Industrial High School
Annemanie, Alabama
Established 1902

Arlington Literary and Industrial High School established in 1902 at Annemanie, Alabama, was the fifth mission school founded in Wilcox County through the Freedmen's Board of the United Presbyterian Church of North America. Annemanie was one of the communities where the County operated a three-months-a-year school for black boys and girls. For that reason, many parents in the area sent their children to other communities where mission schools were located, because the school term was eight months.

Beginning of Annemanie School

In the early 1900s, some of the people in the community decided to ask the Freedmen's Board of the United Presbyterian Church to start a school in their area. Three citizens, Mr. Sam Kimbro, Mr. I. L. Dumas, and Rev. Daniel Davenport, were asked to pursue the idea. The three men petitioned the board for a school and were granted the request based on the condition that the community would donate the land on which to build a school.

The people responded to the idea by purchasing ten acres of land from Mr. Eddie and Mrs. Missouri Robinson. This acreage was connected to the small plot where the one-room schoolhouse stood. The County donated the one-room school and land to the community. One plot of the land lay on the right side of the highway and the other plot lay on the left side of the highway leading from the railroad station toward the Alabama River. A suitable location for the school had now been acquired and the next step was to find an educator to establish the school.

Rev. J. T. Arter, principal and minister at Prairie Institute, a mission school, was asked to move to Arlington, Alabama and take charge of the task. Rev. Arter, a Knoxville College graduate, was described as being highly educated, energetic and suitable for the job. Rev. and Mrs. Arter and their children moved to Arlington in 1900. Putting together ten acres from the community plus an acre with a one-room school there was a nucleus to build a larger building.

Rev. Arter's Vision for the New School
The Arter Plan

Rev. Arter was a great admirer of Booker T. Washington and his work at Tuskegee Institute, so he wanted the Arlington Literary and Industrial School to be patterned after Tuskegee Institute. Rev. Arter visited Tuskegee Institute as much as possible so that he could learn more about its plan and operation. When Rev. Arter returned home from one of his visits to Tuskegee Institute, he had decided to use the Tuskegee Plan as a model because the Tuskegee Plan would allow students to learn a trade along with their academic subjects, preparing them to support themselves in the world of work.

The Tuskegee Plan

In 1902, work began improving the school. The first buildings erected on the school land were a carpenter shop, a blacksmith shop and a home for the vice principal. Using the-one room schoolhouse as a starting point, it was enlarged until there was a chapel and enough rooms to accommodate elementary and high school grades. The men of the community worked untiringly to help accomplish this task. They cut the logs from the ten-acre plot and hauled them to the sawmill by wagon teams, where they were made into lumber and other needed building materials. The chapel would be used for daily chapel exercises, Sabbath School, worship services, Wednesday night prayer meeting and Young Peoples meetings.

After beginning work on the physical plant, Rev. Arter readily came to the conclusion that more land was needed for expansion. By the end of the first year's work, the board bought three farms in the surrounding area. They were the Cook farm, The Beck farm and the Pearson place. This was a very wise investment because there were two large buildings on the Cook farm. The two-story building was used to accommodate the principal and his family, the teachers and a small number of girls. The one-story building housed the young boys and a matron. On the Beck farm was a large two-story house which accommodated the older boys. The Pearson place provided logs which were sawed into boards, shingles and heavy timbers and were used to construct other buildings.

ARLINGTON LITERARY AND INDUSTRIAL HIGH SCHOOL, ITS NAME AND LOCATION

The following information about the Arlington School was told to me by Mr. Johnny Southall, a native and lifetime resident of that community.

The property of the school was divided by a highway. One side was known as Arlington and the other side was Annemanie. A portion of the school campus was situated on the Arlington side and a portion on the Annemanie side. A boardwalk connected the two sides of the school campus. The post office was located on the left side. The school was named Arlington Literary and Industrial High School and received its mail from the Annemanie Post Office. The check below shows this particular information.

ORIGIN OF THE NAME ANNEMANIE

It has been handed down by word of mouth that Annemanie was named by a certain citizen of that area who was the father of twin daughters whom he named Anne and Manie. Putting the two names together as one, the father named Annemanie after his twin daughters. The name Annemanie is often spelled different ways, but school records as early as 1901 show the spelling as Annemanie.

THE FACULTY

The faculty members, most of whom were Knoxville College graduates, came from various locations in and out of the state. Most of them were only normal school graduates. During that particular era, the term "normal school graduate" was used to identify persons who had graduated from high school. These individuals served as role models and exerted wholesome influence on the students.

THE FIRST YEAR OF SCHOOL

The first year of school was 1903-1904. That year only local students were taught by only two teachers, Rev. John T. Arter and Mr. George Johnson.

GROWTH AND EXPANSION OF THE SCHOOL

After acquiring the Cook, Beck and Pearson farms, there was plenty of room for improvements and expansions. Using the Tuskegee Plan as its guide, many trade and industrial courses were set up at the school to be taught along with the academic courses. For the girls, there were domestic science classes. Girls were taught plain sewing, dressmaking, homemaking, preparing and serving meals and table setting. The first task to complete in the plain sewing class required the girls to make their graduating dresses when they completed the high school curriculum. These dresses were made of white organdy material.

The trades for the male students were carpentry, blacksmithing, brick making, farming and sawmill work. The largest numbers of students were engaged in farming, where they learned to clear the land for planting crops, rotate crops, terrace hillsides and cultivate the crops with the most up-to-date equipment.

The trades of carpentry, sawmilling, and blacksmithing not only supplied the needs of the school but brought in extra revenue for the school. Lumber was sold and the carpentry and blacksmithing departments supplied service to the community and others for a fee. The classes in carpentry constructed a potato house, a green house, a large barn and a belfry. The lumber was supplied by the classes in sawmilling. Probably, the most important trade was farming because it supplied food for the boarding departments. The farm supplied vegetables and fruits and farm animals (cattle and hogs) were raised to supplement the meat supply.

THE WORK PLAN FOR STUDENTS

The work to maintain the school plant and to provide food for the boarding departments was done by students. Teachers taught the skills and supervised the work. A work schedule consisted of one hour's work daily Monday through Friday, and two hour's work on Saturdays. To help students working their way through school, summer school and night classes were held. Oftentimes to attract more highly skilled and efficient teachers, they were given free room and board.

Students Work Card

From 7 a. m. to 5 p. m.

NAME

Has done work satisfactory

Teacher

Note---A mark on card will indicate ti ness.

Student Work Card used during the Arter Years
Arlington Literary & Industrial School

THE NEW GIRLS' DORMITORY

Around the year 1908, there was a pressing need for a new girls' dormitory. The Board of Missions allowed Rev. Arter to open an office in Pittsburgh, Pennsylvania to present the needs of the work of the church and school and to make solicitations for funds. From this effort enough funds were donated to build a new dorm. It is said that a very large structure, containing bedrooms, bathrooms, offices, a laundry, a well-equipped kitchen, a cannery, a large dining room and running water, was constructed. The new dorm was named Gowan hall in honor of Mrs. Gowan who donated one thousand dollars to the construction fund.

After the completion of the dorm, the school was advertised widely. Students came from Montgomery, Birmingham, Demopolis, Selma, Mobile and many smaller cities and rural areas of Wilcox County. Students also came from states as far away as South Carolina, Illinois, Tennessee, Pennsylvania, Georgia and Mississippi.

DAILY ACTIVITIES FOR THE NEW GIRLS' DORMITORY

Although the new dorm was designated as a girls' dorm, it would also house some of the female teachers. Rev. Arter had in mind a specific plan for the occupants of the building. This time, he wanted the new facility to be patterned after the Boarding Department of Knoxville College.

The plan called for a homelike atmosphere. Students and teachers would eat together in the spacious dining room three times a day, giving them opportunity for fellowship and interaction. Twice a day, mornings and evenings, they would have family worship consisting of singing Psalms, scripture reading and prayer. The students lined up and marched in and out of the dining room at mealtime. The meals were prepared by students who were taught to prepare and serve meals.

In 1911, the first twelfth grade class graduated. The class had two students, one female, Elizabeth Kimbro Jasper, and one male, Joseph S. Hope.

For a period of years, according to research during the Arter years, grades 11 and 12 were discontinued for several years. The two grades were re-added in later years.

MRS. ELIZABETH KIMBRO JASPER

Mrs. Elizabeth Kimbro Jasper, a young woman from the community, lived in the home of Rev. & Mrs. Arter while attending school at Arlington Literary and Industrial School. After graduating, she attended Knoxville College. She became a teacher and taught for five years in the Alabama Missions.

MR. JOSEPH S. HOPE

After graduating from the Arlington Mission, Mr. Hope attended Tuskegee Institute and graduated in 1913 in Vocational Agriculture. He later studied at Hampton Institute in Virginia. Mr. Hope taught Vocational Agriculture at Snow Hill Institute in Alabama and in Dallas County. He was a farm agent in Russell County, Alabama and the farm manager at Arlington Literary and Industrial High School. In 1922, he and his wife moved to Little Rock, Arkansas, where he taught Vocational Agriculture at Pulaski County Training School and Magnolia Training School in Magnolia, Arkansas.

STUDENT BEHAVIOR

The Arlington School was founded on the principles of education and Bible training. Students were given special training in good behavior and good manners. Personal appearance was always at its best. The principal,

Rev. James T. Arter, was a great role model. A former student commented about Rev. Arter in the following manner: "Rev. Arter was always busy, never missed a chapel exercise, always dressed to perfection and was a great role model."

GROWTH AND INFLUENCE OF THE SCHOOL

The work of the mission grew steadily and rapidly. Before the end of the third boarding year, the dormitories were filled to capacity. Large numbers of applications were received for admission to the boarding departments, but due to the lack of accommodations, many were turned away.

Arlington Literary and Industrial School, located at Annemanie because of its mission design, became a great institution for education and Bible training. The campus was a place of beauty and well kept at all times. Parents, visitors and friends were always welcome. Members from the Presbyterian Board who visited the campus in the early years were Dr. R. W. McGranahan, Rev. Ralph McCollough and Mrs. Ray Shear.

THE ARTER YEARS

Rev. and Mrs. Arter began their work at the Arlington School in 1900 and remained there through the spring of 1918.

Mrs. Arter summed up their years of service in the following manner:

"Arlington Literary and Industrial Institute at its peak had more than one hundred fifty boarding students and a faculty numbering between twenty-five to thirty persons. The school was a large, healthy, happy family with a wholesome atmosphere of security and contentment, together with a high moral standard where clean, personal living prevailed. The prevalence of this atmosphere can be attributed to the influence of the lives of the teachers and workers, a wholesome recreational program, the regular services of the church, and the family Altar in the home school."

Following Rev. Arter, Rev. Richard P. Williams was named principal and pastor of the mission. He took over the reins in the fall of 1918. During his administration, the Board of National Missions financed the construction of a new administration building. The Wilcox County Board of Education constructed a Vocational Agriculture building under the Smith Hughes Act in 1935. The National Board financed a new boys' dorm and the County added a gymnasium. Home Economics and Vocational Agriculture were added to the curriculum.

With the addition of a new academic building to the campus, a new chapel for church services was added as well. The boarding departments continued and students continued to come from places outside the county. The school and church continued its mission of education and Bible training for its students. At the close of the school year of 1945, Rev. Richard P. Williams retired and returned to his native home of Virginia. Rev. Williams served as principal and pastor from 1918 to 1945, a total of twenty-seven years.

Mr. Walter Sutton, a Selma, Alabama native and a Knoxville College graduate, became principal of Arlington Literary and Industrial School. The County began paying most of the faculty members with the exception of Bible and Domestic Science teachers, lunchroom workers and the janitor, who were still paid by the National Board of Missions.

Professor K. P. Thomas, a native of Snow Hill, Alabama and a graduate of Tuskegee Institute, became the principal. It was during Mr. Thomas's leadership that most teachers were paid by the County Board of Education. The Bible teacher, a plain sewing teacher, a janitor and a maintenance worker continued to be paid by the Nation Board. Arlington Literary and Industrial High School became Annemanie High School.

Principals received a supplement from the board for supervision of its property. The facilities at the Annemanie High School, except for a gym and the Vocational Building, were still owned by the Presbyterian National Board, which maintained the upkeep of the property.

The school continued its work and made great progress, but soon major changes would take place which would affect the schools of Wilcox County because of the ruling of the United States Supreme Court in the case of Brown versus the Board of Education. The Supreme Court ruled that racial segregation in public schools is unconstitutional.

Professor K. P. Thomas was the last principal to serve the Annemanie High School. He became principal in 1949 and maintained the position until 1971, a period of twenty-two years.

CLOSING OF THE ANNEMANIE SCHOOL

The Wilcox County Board of Education, mandated by Federal Law to integrate its public school system discontinued the high school in 1968 and began transporting the students to Pine Hill Consolidated School in Pine Hill, Alabama. The Elementary Department remained at Annemanie until 1971. At the end of the 1971 school year, the Elementary School was closed and students were transported to Pine Hill in the fall of 1971.

The following document is a copy of a written account of the transition, the Exchange of Property between the Wilcox County Board of Education and the Board of National Missions. Excerpts from the minutes dated March 20, 1971.

The Superintendent explained to the Board that in negotiating with Mr. Peter A. Hall, Attorney at Law, for an exchange of property between the

County Board of Education, to approve this transfer and convey to the Board of National Missions of the United Presbyterian Church in the United States of America the property named above with description attached.

Two buildings on the Annemanie campus were constructed by the Board of Education, namely the Vocational and Home Economic Building and gymnasium.

The following letter to Mr. McLean Pitts regarding consolidation of Annemanie School dated September 20, 1971 was read to the Board and the same was unanimously approved:

Mr. McLean Pitts
Pitts, Pitts and Thompson
Attorneys at Law
City National Bank Building
Selma, Alabama

Dear Mr. Pitts:

Re: Consolidation of Annemanie School

On Friday afternoon at 3 o'clock our maintenance man, Mr. Clyde Champion, went to Annemanie School and carried his seven man maintenance crew and four county trucks. Immediately after the dismissal of students, he started the removal of the Wilcox County equipment from the Annemanie School and transferred same.

Arlington Literary and Industrial High School began in 1902 and continued serving until 1971, a span of seventy years. The mission schools served its students well and gave great Christian and professional foundations which equipped its students to serve others. The service of the school bears out the motto: The elevator to success is not running; take the stairs.

ARLINGTON LITERARY AND INDUSTRIAL HIGH SCHOOL

Principals/Pastors

Rev. J. T. Arter - Principal/Pastor	1900-1918
Rev. Richard Williams - Principal/Pastor	1918-1945
Professor Walter Sutton - Principal	1945-1949
Professor K. P. Thomas - Principal	1949-1971
(Annemanie)	

Other ministers who served the Arlington Congregation

Dr. C. C. Brown	1945-1963
Rev. Benjamin Thompson	1963-1995

Rev. J. T. Arter
Principal & Pastor
Prairie Institute 1894-1900
Arlington Literary and Industrial High School 1900-1918

Reverend Richard P. Williams
Principal, Pastor
Arlington Literary & Industrial High School 1918-1945

Girls' Dormitory
Annemanie, Alabama

Boys' Dormitory
Annemanie, Alabama

Reverend Dr. C. C. Brown
Minister for Arlington and Prairie Congregations
1945 - 1963

Arlington Literary and Industrial High School
Annemanie, Alabama

K. P. Thomas

CHAPTER VI

MIDWAY MISSION
Midway, Alabama
Established 1903

Midway Mission, the last United Presbyterian School to be established in Wilcox County, was founded in 1903. Midway was situated on the side of the Alabama River beginning exactly at that boundary line and extending to the boundary line of Prairie. Mr. Thomas P. Marsh, a graduate of Knoxville College, became principal of this elementary school grades 1-6. It has been said that the budget for the Midway School for one year was $1,080.00. The school enrollment was 120 pupils and the number of teachers was three.

Very recently, two sisters, Mrs. Annie Ross Kennedy and Mrs. Nancy Ross Pettway, related to me that their father, Mr. Will Ross, who was born and reared in the Midway Community, was a product of the mission school. Mrs. Lula Marsh Wardell, sister of Professor Marsh, was a teacher at Midway School. Mrs. Ludy Gildersleeve, a Lutheran teacher who later taught at the same community, also recalled having been told about the former mission.

The Midway Mission activities were carried on in the same manner as the other Presbyterian Missions in Wilcox County.

Rev. D. F. White, minister at Prairie, also served the Midway Church.

Mrs. Lula D. Marsh Wardell
A teacher at Midway
A 100th Birthday Party was held
March 1978
St. Paul's A.M.E. Church
Cleveland, Ohio

Professor Thomas P. Marsh, Sr.
Principal of Midway Mission
1903 -

45

Chapter VII

The Campus Sites and Buildings

The school sites were always interesting places. The buildings and grounds were well kept. All buildings were constructed mainly of wood but were kept painted inside and out and well repaired.

Campus sites varied in size from several acres to a large number of acres. Arlington Literary and Industrial High School and Prairie Institute had large acreages because farms were part of their programs.

Beautification day was an annual school activity at school sites. On a particular day students and teachers cleaned grounds and buildings, and flowers and trees were planted. If there were wooded fences, they were whitewashed or painted white. The trunks of trees and rocks were also whitewashed. Students were taught the importance of well-kept surroundings, beauty and cleanliness, a lesson which could prove helpful in life.

Visitors

The campuses were often frequented by visitors. Visitors from the United Presbyterian Board included Dr. Witherspoon, secretary of the board, Dr. R. W. McGranahan, Mrs. Ray Shear and Dr. J. S. McCullouch, President of Knoxville College. Parents and friends were welcomed and encouraged to visit the schools on a regular basis.

Student School Supplies

Parents were required to buy textbooks for their children. Books were not changed or revised with any regularity, so if a family of several children purchased a set of books, they could be passed from one child to another for many years. There were no libraries but these came in later years. Parents furnished paper and pencils for their children. Very often children could be seen wearing a string around the neck with a pencil attached. This was a preventive measure to keep from losing the pencil. A lot of times, the child carried a tablet of rough paper with a picture of a parrot wearing shoes that were too big. The tablet was named, "A Polly Parrot Tablet."

The Daily Devotion

No school day was complete without holding Daily Devotion. Each school selected its own time frame, which was usually in the morning. The principal conducted the devotion, which consisted of hymn singing, scripture, prayer and a short message. The second part of the devotion was given over to the discussion and reminder of rules and regulations followed by announcements. The students lined up in their classrooms and marched in and out of the chapel. Students were required to be very quiet and orderly for this activity. All students and teachers were required to attend. The procedure of holding Daily Devotion was discarded about the same time when daily Bible lessons were discontinued and prayer was banned from public schools.

Music in the Curriculum

Special emphasis was placed on learning to sing and enjoy beautiful music. Singing was given special attention and all students were expected to participate. Hymns, patriotic songs, spirituals and folk music were taught. Choirs, soloist and high school bands were trained. The true American folksongs, the Negro Spirituals, were taught and sung without any instrument. The human voices blended in sweet harmony as the spirituals were sung.

Over a long period of years, many music teachers were employed but I particularly wish to mention two of them by name. Miss Lillian Douglass from Birmingham, Alabama taught at Prairie Institute as a fifth grade teacher and also a music teacher. She played both piano and cello. Mrs. Helen Auhorn from Pennsylvania was employed at Miller's Ferry Normal School as a music teacher and secretary. She was a violinist as well.

THE STUDENT POPULATION

The schools grew very rapidly. Boarding departments were filled to capacity. Students from far and near came to take advantage of the excellent mission schools and a school year of eight months. They came from Marengo, Dallas and Clark counties. They came from cities as well as rural areas. Mobile, Selma, Birmingham, Demopolis and Montgomery sent students. Students came from Georgia, Florida and Mississippi. Various individual records show that pupils came from South Carolina, Illinois, Pennsylvania and Tennessee. Some parents sent their children to live with relatives in the communities where mission schools were located. The largest number of students were the children of Wilcox, where the schools were located.

In several cases, adult students went back to high school to get a high school diploma after they had passed middle age. To attend high school at Miller's Ferry, a certain lady, Mrs. Susie Cheesboro, drove her horse and buggy for transportation to and from school, a round trip of about fourteen miles.

One student related this story telling how she and her younger sister and brother made their trek to Miller's Ferry Normal and Industrial School in the early twenties. The two sisters and brother were born in Choctaw County. Their parents put them on a boat traveling from Womack Hill to Jackson, Alabama on the Tombigbee River. They spent the night in Jackson, Alabama with an aunt. The next day they were put on the train to Catherine, Alabama, where they were met and were carried to Miller's Ferry. They accomplished their goal because all three graduated from high school at Miller's Ferry.

SCHOOL CURRICULUMS

All six missions were referred to as sister schools; therefore they shared a common curriculum. To begin, Bible can be called the number one subject and it was taught daily with great emphasis in grades 1-12. No child was exempted from Bible study. Bible was taught.

In the early years, Prairie Institute was grade 1-9, Midway was grade 1-6, Canton Bend, Miller's Ferry and Camden Academy were grades 1-8, Arlington began with grades 1-12 but for a short period of time dropped grades 11 and 12, picking them up again later. The curriculum for grades 1-9 consisted of Bible study, arithmetic, reading, English, spelling and geography, with the addition of domestic sciences, sewing and cooking. Music was taught in all grades. Prairie Institute, Miller's Ferry and Annemanie taught shop classes. Exactly what the shop classes consisted of was not described.

Miller's Ferry became a high school in 1918, Camden Academy in 1930 and Arlington, which was founded as a high school, returned to that status later. These schools offered the same curriculum for grades 1-9 as mentioned earlier. The high schools offered math, algebra, history, Latin, science and Cicero. Each high school offered English, history, science courses, math courses, home economics, and agriculture courses beginning in 1930. Foreign languages were taught. Prairie offered Latin, Miller's Ferry Normal and Industrial High offered Latin, Cicero, Greek and French.

Each school had a music teacher with such responsibilities as preparing a choir, preparing musical numbers for all special programs, and playing for daily chapel exercise and worship services. Some teachers were capable of teaching other kinds of music such as band, violin and cello. Students who were interested in piano lessons and whose parents were able to pay a small monthly fee were given private lessons.

Music as an important phase helped students who went on to become teachers to give their classes some musical training and appreciation for good music. Two schools, Camden Academy and Miller's Ferry, trained bands. Mrs. Tillie E. Johnson, who also founded the hospital at Miller's Ferry Normal and Industrial School, trained a band. Arlington Literary and Industrial School had an orchestra and a band.

TUITION

The schools did require parents to pay a very small tuition on a monthly basis for their children, and that was on a graduated basis according to grade. If parents could not pay money, various farm products such as hay, corn, sweet potatoes, molasses and other produce was accepted in lieu of money.

DISCIPLINE

Today when addressing school discipline the term "zero tolerance" is often quoted. Mission schools functioned quite effectively with zero tolerance. While spanking or switching could be used, other methods were employed as well. Many a male student was sent to round up the coal pile or plant trees. Girls and boys alike could be given time out by standing in the corner of the room or sitting by the teacher's desk with their back turned to the rest of their classmates. Misbehavior or failing to prepare one's school work could also result in a student getting his work during recess or being kept for a short period of time after school. Of course, buses came into use later and staying after school was discontinued.

Another phase of discipline emphasized from elementary grades through high school was character building. Reading of good books and good poetry was one of the methods used to instill good character. Memorizing poetry was an exciting procedure for character building. Examples of such poetry used in elementary grades are recorded below.

Poems

One Thing at a Time

Work while you work,
Play while you play
That is the way
To be happy and gay.

All that you do
Do with your might
Things done by halves
Are never done right.
One thing each time
And that done well,
Is a very good rule
As many can tell.

Moments are useless
Trifled away,
So work while you work
And play while you play.

by M. A. Stodant

Who Hath a Book

Who hath a book
Hath friends at hand,
And gold and gear
At his command;
And rich estates
If he but look
Are held by him
Who hath a book.
Has but to read,
And he may be
A King indeed;
His Kingdom is
His inglenook,
All this is his
Who hath a book.

Do Your Best

Do the very best you can
Never be a "halfway man."
Even though' the task is light,
Work at it with all your might.

Every hour throughout the day,
Do your best in every way.

When you have a task to do,
Never fail to see it through.

by Esther Lee Carter

Effort

There's something in a task well done
That cannot be explained.
A singing in our heart all day,
From some fine goal attained.
So it is not worthwhile for you,
To work with all your might
On any task that you should do
And see that it's done right?

For I am sure that you will find
When once you have begun,
That honest effort brings success
And with it work well done.

by Esther Lee Carter

A Rule for Living

Do all the good you can
By all the means you can
In all the ways you can
In all the places you can
At all the times you can
To all the people you can
As long as ever you can.

by John Wesley

Four Things

Four things a man must learn to do,
If he would make his record true.
To think without confusion clearly,
To love his fellow-man sincerely,
To act from honest motives purely,
To trust in God and heaven sincerely.

by Dr. Henry Van Dyke

Make new friends, but keep the old.
The new are silver, the old are gold.

by Joseph Parry

The whole truth of a kind deed lies in the love that inspires it.

by The Talmud

Thank God every morning when you get up, that you have something to do that day which must be done whether you like it or not. Being forced to work and forced to do your best will breed in you temperance and self-control, diligence and strength of will, cheerfulness, and content, and a hundred virtues which the idle never knew.

HEATING SYSTEMS

The early heating systems in the schools differed, perhaps because no two schools were ever built at the same time. They did, however, fall into two categories. The earliest method used the pot belly stove which burned coal and wood. Each summer the school principal ordered the year's supply of coal and wood for the winter. Consequently each school had a coal pile and a wood pile. The second heating system added was steam heat. A boiler which used water, coal, and a radiator system supplied the steam heat. A trained individual was responsible for firing the boiler. That individual usually began his task around four o'clock each morning or kept the boiler running all night when the weather was very cold.

THE BOARDING DEPARTMENT

Boarding departments were essential to the life of the schools because of the long distances between schools. Five of the mission schools had boarding departments for girls and boys. During the early years of the schools, boarding departments were added to the campus layout. These building were generally filled to capacity because they accommodated both students and teachers.

To live in the dormitory required a monthly fee called a boarding fee which both teachers and students were required to pay. Some students who could not meet the money requirement were given the opportunity to work out their board. The jobs included preparing meals, doing laundry, cleaning classrooms or other buildings, starting fires in classrooms, chapel or church, farm work or helping in the principal's home. The second option to pay board allowed parents to pay with farm products which could be used to prepare meals for students and teachers who resided in the dormitories.

RECREATION AND SPORTS

Each school had a planned social and recreational program which in the early years did not include dancing and playing cards.

At social events, games were played or students sat and held conversations. The main feature was the Grand March. That was as close to dancing as one could get. Corners were squared as you marched. The march always ended with the special feature called the Grand Left and Right March. Refreshments were served. Quite often, on a beautiful Sunday afternoon, a faculty member would carry the boarding girls for a nice walk or visit a sick, elderly person.

Baseball, basketball and football were the main sports. Baseball was the oldest of the three. Running track became very popular at Camden Academy. Students participated in various track meets throughout the state and oftentimes were winners in the events. One Camden Academy student traveled to Europe to compete in the Olympics.

Camden Academy and Miller's Ferry had football teams and they were great rivals. One particular time when the two schools met in competition, a Miller's Ferry student suffered a broken leg. Annemanie's principle sport was baseball. It has been said that one Miller's Ferry football coach told his team, "Whatever you do, beat Camden Academy."

A great variety of ring games were very popular in the elementary grades. Other games included hopscotch, marbles, horseshoes and ball played with a rubber ball.

GRADUATION AND BACCALAUREATE DAYS

These two days were the high drama days of a student's school career. After twelve years of continuous study and completion of one's curriculum, students looked forward with joy and great anticipation to Baccalaureate Sunday and graduation exercises.

Schools ninth grade and below held only graduation exercises, whereas the high schools became accustomed to holding baccalaureate exercises on the last Sunday of the school term, followed by commencement exercises several days later.

A lot of preparation was made with students and teachers participating in making the preparations. Special music was prepared, two speakers of renown were invited, one for baccalaureate and one for commencement. The campus and building were made spick and span. For a couple of weeks preceding the programs, practice was held daily so that the exercises would be graceful and inspiring. Every class had a class motto.

For these special occasions, faculty and class marched into the school's chapel, with faculty first followed by the class. At the end of the program, only the class marched out.

The most important phase of the commencement program was the awarding of diplomas. Students who reached this accomplishment exhibited a great spirit of happiness. To climax the program, if there was a school song, it was sung by the students and audience.

People who attended these special programs were parents, grandparents, young siblings, former graduates and family friends.

During the early years, students entered the world of work, but as time progressed, students began to go into higher education.

After completing many years in school, students became teachers, nurses, ministers, post office workers, blacksmiths, carpenters, doctors, lawyers, college presidents, college professors, music teachers, hospital administrators, and many entered the armed services and gained ranks such as corporal, major, captain and others.

CHAPTER VIII

ESTABLISHMENT OF UNITED PRESBYTERIAN CONGREGATIONS

The Founding of United Presbyterian Churches in Wilcox County

Wherever a mission was established, provision was always made for a place of worship, but there were no United Presbyterian congregations fully connected through the Presbytery, Senate, Synod and General Assembly. After Rev. Johnson completed his task of reviewing the work at the Miller's Ferry Mission, he reported to the Freedmen's Board that there was no United Presbyterian Church accessible to colored people in this area and a church was needed for the good of the work here.

The message was conveyed to the board in the form of a petition signed by ten people. "The individuals were: Rev. C. H. Johnson, P. C, Cloud, Col. English, Amp Madison, Charles Swan, Mrs. P. C. Cloud, Mrs. Sarah English, Mrs. Elizabeth Madison, Miss T. E. Scott, Miss L. E. Jarnigan." (p. 7)

The board responded with a favorable reply and Rev. Johnson was given authority to organize the church.

Founding of the Miller's Ferry Church

After worship services on December 24, 1893, the congregation was organized with Rev. Johnson as moderator. It began with two members and these two members were elected the first elders. The church grew rapidly increasing in numbers.

The school and chapel suffered a great tragedy on May 4, 1895. Both buildings were destroyed by fire. The congregation now had no meeting place for worship, but Shady Grove Baptist Church of Miller's Ferry came to their aid by offering them the use of the Baptist Church until Miller's Ferry could rebuild their sanctuary. The offer was accepted.

The following report to the Presbytery of Tennessee indicates the growth of the church from 1893 to 1896. "The report was as follows:

> Communicants 54, Contributions: Foreign mission $5.00, Church
> Extension $5.00, Freedmen's Mission $5.00, Home Mission $5.00,
> congregation expenses $313.00, Total contributions $333.00.
>
> Missionary Societies 2, Young People's Society members 52, Sabbath
> School teachers and officers 12, number of pupils 327." (Page 20)

The new congregation received The Lord's Supper for the first time on March 12, 1894. Miller's Ferry was the first United Presbyterian Church for colored people in Wilcox County, Alabama.

Establishment of the Prairie Church

The year was 1898 and Rev. Arter continued his work as pastor and principal of Prairie Institute. During the month of December, Rev. Arter invited the Miller's Ferry Church to join the Prairie Church on the second Sunday of the month to help in starting a new congregation at Prairie.

Worship services were held, and after the services the Miller's Ferry Session met along with Rev. Arter to take

Beginnings in the Black Belt and Short Stories of the Lives of Dr. Charles Henry and Mrs. Tillie E. Johnson by Mrs. Sophia D. Johnson Pp. 7, 20 copyright 1940

in members in the church. A list of fourteen names was submitted to the session and received into the church. This was the beginning of the Prairie Church.

The date is March 19, 1899. The Miller's Ferry United Presbyterian Church meets with the Prairie Congregation and ten people are received into the church.

On the following Sunday, the Miller's Ferry Congregation meets with the Prairie Church and ten more members were added. The membership now totals thirty four. The meeting closes with a sermon by Rev. C. H. Johnson followed by prayer.

The Prairie Church is now the second United Presbyterian Church in Wilcox County.

United Presbyterian Congregation of Midway

Midway Mission was built with a combination chapel and school. Because the school was discontinued early, no separate church was erected, but it is known that Rev. D. F. White pastored the church during the same years he was the minister at the Prairie Church.

The Canton Bend Church

No exact date for the founding of the Canton Bend Church is presently known, however, it is known that Rev. J. N. Cotton served as the first minister. The ministers who followed Rev. Cotton were Rev. D. F. White and Rev. James F. Reese.

The Arlington Church

The following paragraphs are written in the record of Arlington Literary Industrial School:

A school and chapel were constructed on the campus 1903-04. In this chapel religious activities and services were held. No exact date is given as to when the congregation was established.

The second statement mentioned that in the course of time a church was organized to which many teachers and students joined themselves. Many teachers and workers paid tithes.

The Camden Church

The Camden United Presbyterian Church is said to have been established between 1900 and 1905. We do know that the school chapel served as the sanctuary during the early years of the church.

In 1952, a church building was erected on the campus at Camden Academy. Rev. James Foster Reese, a graduate of Knoxville College and Pittsburgh, Pennsylvania, was called to serve as minister of the newly constructed church. The church was given the name Trinity United Presbyterian Church.

In 1958, Rev. Reese accepted a call to Knoxville College to become minister of the church located on the campus. Rev. Thomas L. Threadgill, a Morehouse College graduate and a recipient of a Divinity Degree from Pittsburgh Xenia Seminary, was called by the Trinity Church congregation. He accepted the call and began his work there in 1959.

With their pastor, Trinity Presbyterian Church served well the community and the student body for some fourteen years. With the coming of the civil rights movement, the church experienced a great change. The Wilcox County Board of Education exercised the right of Eminent Domain and seized the property owned by the Board of National Missions. This included the land on which Trinity Presbyterian Church was built. Trinity Church was torn down and the congregation became united with the Miller's Ferry Church.

The church did not remain at Miller's Ferry. The congregation purchased a new site in Camden, Alabama and erected a new church. The church was built in 1970 and dedicated in October 1971 under the name New Trinity Presbyterian Church.

CHAPTER IX

A DAY AT CHURCH

A day at church began with devotion followed by classes which were organized by grades and were taught by your regular day school teachers. Sunday School was followed by worship services which consisted of singing hymns, reading of scriptures, an anthem by the choir and a sermon by the minister. Communion was given on a designated Sunday.

CHURCH ACTIVITIES

Church activities among the congregations were very similar. Sabbath School convened every Sunday the year round. Worship services were held each Sunday at some churches and others twice per month. Church choirs were a permanent feature. Each school had a music teacher who was responsible for the church music. The choirs practiced and sang beautiful anthems at Church services. Other religious activities included prayer meeting on Wednesday night and special programs during the year at Christmas, Easter, Thanksgiving, Mother's Day and Children's Day.

All boarding students and teachers were expected to attend all church-related programs including Sabbath school, church services and prayer meeting.

CHRISTIAN ORGANIZATIONS

Two special youth groups convened on Sunday evening. They were Young Peoples Christian Union and Junior Missionary Society. Each organization had a teacher sponsor. Both community and boarding students attended the meetings. When a member reached age twelve as a Junior Missionary member, he moved up to the YPCU group. They were eligible to attend that group until they graduated from high school. These groups offered extra Bible training, singing and social activities.

SABBATH SCHOOL AND YOUNG PEOPLE'S CONVENTION

A special program of the church was the annual Sabbath School and Young People's convention. The convention sites were rotated among the churches. The convention was held in the early fall. Delegates were selected to represent their various churches. Young people and adults participated.

Besides being a part of the convention, the young people enjoyed the opportunity to visit all missions and spend a couple of nights, Friday and Saturday, away from home.

These conventions were designed to motivate young people to pursue religious education with greater enthusiasm. The youth participated in Bible contests, writing and reciting orations based on very meaningful topics. There was singing, special music, a social hour and recreational activities. Sabbath School teachers and Sabbath School superintendents were sponsors.

Arlington Literary and Industrial School during the tenure of Rev. Arter had a very excellent music department. Along with the regular music teacher, other teachers would organize and direct singing groups. There was both a band and an orchestra. For church services the choir was accompanied by an organist, and wind and string instruments.

REVIVALS

Revivals were held when schools were in session during the winter months. This provided the minister the opportunity to preach to the student bodies and continue their Bible training. Revival in the winter season was unheard of in the surrounding churches. One minister is said to have remarked, "I never saw people run the devil in the winter time." Church services here held at night to accommodate the community. Revival lasted for one week.

THANK OFFERING

Thank offering was a special feature of the church program. Around the Thanksgiving season each year, a Thanksgiving program was given and a special collection was lifted. If an adult was able, he or she contributed at least $3.65, a penny per day. Children gave whatever amount given them by their parents.

Children brought their offerings in attractive colored boxes and grown-ups used specially prepared envelopes. The funds were sent to the Board to help support the mission work of the Junior Missionary Society.

THE HYMNBOOKS

Hymnals - Throughout the years, several different hymnals were used for all religious activities.

The Psalter Song Book - Published in Pittsburgh, Pennsylvania by the United Presbyterian Board of Publication in 1895.

The Bible Songs Hymnal - Because its backs were red, it was often called the Red-backed Hymnal. Published in Pittsburgh, Pennsylvania, August 1927.

Songs for Christian Worship - Was published by the board of Christian Education of the United Presbyterian Church in 1950. It was referred to as the Green-backed Hymnal because it had green backs.

The Hymnbook - Published by Presbyterian Church in the United States, Reform Church in America - Presbyterian Church of North America, copyright 1946 and 1956.

The most recent hymnal is the Presbyterian Hymnal - Hymns, Psalms, and Spirituals, published by Westminster John Knox Press, Louisville, Kentucky, 1990.

OTHER AMENITIES PROVIDED BY THE CHURCH

The spirit of the church to help the needy was manifested in at least three other important ways.

Christmas gifts for children were provided by churches and Women Missionary Societies. These gifts consisted of new toys, new clothing and new books. A lot of children received gifts who otherwise would not have but for the generosity of faithful Christians.

Another special gift to the various communities was the contribution of used clothing. This clothing was shipped to the missions in barrels and was referred to as "Barrel Clothes." Families who lost their possessions due to fire, families with large numbers of children or any needy persons were donated the used clothing.

Another viable feature was the scholarship program. Selected students received scholarships, particularly to Presbyterian Colleges. These scholarships provided opportunity for a lot of students to pursue higher education, which they might not have received except for this help.

United Presbyterian Sabbath School and Young Peoples' Convention

at

Arlington Literary and Industrial Institute

Annemanie, Alabama

November 11-12, 1939

CONVENTION THEME: Build With Christ

C. D. McCall, President.

Miss N. A. Davis, Secretary.

Pritchett Printing Co., 1431 Lapsley St., Selma, Ala.

Program

SATURDAY MORNING—NOVEMBER 11th

9:00 Registration ------ Arlington
9:30 Devotion ------ Arlington
Welcome Address ------ Arlington
Response ------ President C. D. McCall
Music ------ Arlington
10:00 Address ------ Rev. R. P. Williams
10:20 Music ------ Camden
10:25 Children's Hour ------ Arlington
10:45 Bible Story Contest ------
11:20 CONFERENCE
(a) Reports ------ S. S. and Y. P. C. U.
(b) Methods ------ S. S. and Y. P. C. U.
(c) The Social Life of S. S. and Y. P. C. U.
11:55 ANNOUNCEMENTS

AFTERNOON SESSION

2:00 Devotion ------ Camden
2:10 Bible Reading Contest.
2:35 Music ------ Prairie
2:40 ROUNDTABLE DISCUSSION: Build With Christ.
(a) Physical Life ------ W. R. Sutton
(b) Mental Life ------ Wm. Patton

Program

(c) Moral Life ------ Wm. Peters
(d) Spiritual Life ------ Reuben Yancy
3:05 Music (Congregation)
3:10 ANNOUNCEMENTS
3:20 RECREATION: B. T. Ridgeway—Miss T. E. Howse

EVENING SESSION

7:00 Devotion ------ Miller's Ferry
7:10 Business
7:45 Music ------ Miller's Ferry
7:50 Oratorical Contest ------ Building With Christ
8:15 Music.
8:20 ANNOUNCEMENTS

SABBATH MORNING

9:30 Devotion ------ Canton Bend
9:40 Sabbath School
Male Class ------ I. V. Elligan
Female Class ------ Mrs. B. B. Groves
10:20 RECESS
10:30 Pulpit devotion and introduction of speaker ------ Rev. R. P. Williams
11:00 Sermon ------ Rev. D. F. White
Business
Doxology

Each organization is asked to bring 25c registration fee.

CHAPTER X

STATUS OF CHURCHES AND SCHOOLS TODAY

Six United Presbyterian Churches were established in Wilcox County in the late 19th century and the early 20th century. Today, only three of the congregations remain. They are Arlington Presbyterian at Annemanie, Alabama, New Trinity Presbyterian at Camden, and Prairie Presbyterian Chapel at Prairie, Alabama.

To date, all churches have either been torn down or destroyed by fire. The only original church building remaining is located at Prairie and it is still used as a place of worship.

After almost ninety years of providing schools and support to the education of black boys and girls in Wilcox, all schools established by the United Presbyterians of North America have become a part of the Wilcox County Public School System. From 1884 until 1930, a period of forty-six years, except for Snow Hill Institute, Camden Academy, Miller's Ferry Normal and Industrial High and Arlington Literary and Industrial High Schools were the only high schools for blacks in the county. Only one original mission school building still stands and is in usable condition at Prairie, Alabama. The Arlington School was destroyed by fire in 1969. The chapel and school buildings at Miller's Ferry are in total decay. Canton Bend School and Chapel were destroyed by fire in 1952. The Camden Academy School was condemned by the Board of Education and torn down. There is no known available record concerning the Midway Mission after it was discontinued. Prairie Institute was discontinued in 1969 and students were bused to Miller's Ferry and Wilcox Training School at Miller's Ferry. The school building at Prairie is the only original school which is still standing. The building is kept in repair and used for various community activities.

For years the principals were responsible for the upkeep of the property, with all repairs paid for by the Mission Board. After 1945, the National Board gave Dr. Claude C. Brown of Selma, Alabama, the responsibility to maintain its property. In turn, Mr. Henry Gragg was hired to perform all necessary maintenance work. This procedure was kept up until the County Board assumed full responsibility for all schools.

CHAPTER XI

ESTABLISHMENT OF THE CORPORATION
THE UNITED PRESBYTERIANS OF WILCOX COUNTY, INC.

The United Presbyterian Churches of Wilcox are striving to continue as far as possible a lot of the work carried on by the church of earlier years. After the closing of the last school, the Board of National Missions still held title to several hundred acres of land and buildings as well.

In 1958, the United Presbyterian Church of North America merged with the Presbyterian Church U. S. A. The Board of National Missions was assigned oversight of the properties and ministries of Wilcox County.

In reassessing its work, the General Assembly of the church urged that all mission work be done locally and mandated its board to dispose of all property not being used in mission work. Reacting to the mandate of the General Assembly, the United Presbyterian Congregations of Wilcox County in consultation with the National Board came together and formed a corporation, The United Presbyterians of Wilcox County, Inc., in 1967. The chief purpose of the corporation is to continue the mission spirit by upholding the spiritual, moral and social ministries of the church.

The Board of National Missions gave UPWC nine acres of land at the Prairie site, and a nine-acre site in Camden on which New Trinity Church is located. Later, the Board of National Missions transferred 330 acres at Annemanie to the Synod of the South. The 330 acres were later transferred to the corporation.

The three churches which united to form the corporation were Arlington, Prairie and New Trinity. The Presbytery of Sheppards and Lapsley, headquartered in Birmingham, was given the responsibility of supporting and overseeing its ministries.

The corporation is presently engaged in several ministries, which are a much needed day care center housed at New Trinity Presbyterian Church, a well established tutoring program housed on the Annemanie campus, a gym and a lighted recreational bowl for sports and other activities, a day camp provided by the Presbytery, and for several summers the Lutheran Ministries has provided a six-week enrichment program.

Four and one-half acres of the Annemanie property was donated to the Arlington congregation for a new church site. The new church was erected and dedicated in 1991.

To date, the corporation has received two HUD grants totaling $750,000. The grants are being used to construct a wetland sewerage system and renovate an old boys' dorm into apartments which will provide housing for families with incomes below the poverty level. The second phase of the grant is a Capacity Grant, which will help the corporation to build to the point that it can offer greater services and generate much-needed funds.

Our mission statement encourages us to fulfill our mission, which is to minister to the needs of people in the name of God.

Chapter XII

Influence of the Mission Schools and Churches of Wilcox County

In reviewing the influence of the mission schools and churches, only one term seems suitable to describe the work of the missions— "immeasurable." Thousands of black boys and girls received academic and religious training at these schools.

The most preferable way to begin to evaluate the mission influences is to review the accomplishments of its products, the students. It seems that wherever these students have gone, they have established themselves as good citizens, Christians and productive individuals. The graduates are scattered all over the United States as well as some foreign countries.

In the early years of the schools there were no libraries and no science labs, but after graduating from high school, many students continued their education and earned advanced degrees, from bachelor of science and bachelor of arts degrees to doctorates in a wide range of educational fields and in the ministry.

From these institutions have come teachers, elementary, high school and college professors, doctors, ministers, nurses, poets, writers, engineers and printers, as well as a moderator of the General Assembly of the old United Presbyterian Church, (UPCUSA). Thrift, Christianity, work and outstanding academic skills have become the hallmark of students trained in the mission tradition.

Chapter XIII

Recognitions

The story of the missions would by no means be complete without giving special recognition and thanks to numerous persons who worked tirelessly in many capacities to help the missions attain their goals. First, we recognize the wives of the pastors and principals. A list of the wives follow: Mrs. Tillie Johnson, Mrs. Nanny Bonner, Mrs. Curtis Simpson, Mrs. N. D. Williams, Mrs. Laura Ridgeway, Mrs. Cotton, Mrs. J. T. Arter, Mrs. Elliot, Mrs. Wade, Mrs. Etoile Peters, Mrs. R. P. Williams, Mrs. Gladys Peoples, Mrs. W. G. Wilson, Mrs. Julia Williams, Mrs. Alberta Thomas, and Mrs. Ralph Sutton.

The second group to consider is the energetic teachers, who not only taught well but served as role models and exerted great influence on their students. To name all of them would be an impossible task, so to all who taught at the mission schools, "Thank you."

All the parents occupy a specific place in the lives of the children because it was their eagerness, sacrifices, desires and trust in God which caused the parents to do what was important and necessary to encourage their offspring to take advantage of each opportunity given them.

It was the Divine Spirit which acted on the heart of Judge William Henderson to request the United Presbyterian Church of North America to become involved in a special way in Wilcox county. For this keen insight and spirit of benevolence, we say, "Thank you."

The Freedmen's Board, The Women's General Missionary Society, the National Mission Board and the United Presbyterian Church of North America are thanked for their insight and their work for the betterment of others. We believe that they were led by the Spirit of Christianity to establish the missions.

Thanks are extended to our parents and all others whose combined the work and prayers that were instrumental in making the work successful.

The years of accomplishments will continue into infamy because they are carved and sustained in the minds and spirits of many generations who were given the opportunity to become the best they could be.

The story of the missions would not be complete without referring to some passages of the Bible which are so applicable and inspiring to this story.

> Jesus said unto him, Thou shalt love the Lord thy God with all thy
> heart, and with all thy soul and with all thy mind. And the second is
> like unto it, Thou shalt love thy neighbor as thy self.
>
> Matthew 22:37 & 39

The scripture verses written above are all about love. Love is the basis for service which is required of those who keep these commandments. They were fulfilled through the work of the missions.

The Last Bell

The time is a day approaching the end of May and the year is 1971. The sound of the mission bell has totally become silent. The United Presbyterian Board of National Missions no longer has any connection with the schools of Wilcox County. The call by the bell physically or in one's imagination rings no more; but does that mean that the years also lay silent? The years of accomplishments will continue to live because they are planted in the minds of past generations.

SUCCESS STORIES

DR. LAURENCE FOSTER

Dr. Foster attended Miller's Ferry Normal and Industrial High School as a boarding student. I became acquainted with his daughter, who resides in Pennsylvania. She said, "My father received an outstanding education from Miller's Ferry. He possessed great qualities of leadership and ability. He presented himself at all times in such a manner that his great characteristics always stood out. My father often talked to me about Miller's Ferry Normal and Industrial High School."

The story of his career is included below.

Dr. Laurence Foster - anthropologist; born in Pensacola, Florida, February 3, 1903; son of Frank Lee and Pearl (Hill) Foster; A. B., Lincoln University, 1926, S. T. B. 1929; Ph. D., University of Pennsylvania, 1931; Married Ella Mae Gibson, June 30, 1936; children - Yvonne Camille, Laurence Foster, Jr. University scholar University of Pennsylvania, 1927-1929; teacher of history Stowe Teachers' College of St. Louis, Missouri, 1929-1932; Chairman of Department of Social Sciences, Lincoln University, Chester Co., Pa.; former research associate University of Pennsylvania Museum; general editor Huxley Publishers, New York City, since 1935; guest lecturer. Museo Nacional de Mexico 1930; special representative of Pan-American Union, Washington, D. C. to Mexico 1930; Dean of Instruction, State Teachers' College, Cheyney, Pa., 1933-37; special representative Biological Abstracts, 1936-37. Field research in Canada, Mexico, and Guatemala, under grant from Columbia University, spring and summer of 1929; grant-in-aid fellow, National Research Council, 1931-32; Executive Director of Pennsylvania State Temporary Commission on the Conditions of the Colored Urban Population (wrote preliminary report of Commission, 1941). Formerly president of the Stevens Housing Corporation; former director of research, National Protestant Council on Higher Education; general editor of the Stackpole Social Science Series, Stackpole Company, Harrisburg, Pa., since 1952. Republican. Presbyterian. Club: Pyramid.

Author: *The Functions of a Graduate School in a Democratic Society,* 1936; also private survey reports of higher educational institutions in Alabama, Arkansas, Connecticut, D. C., Georgia, Illinois, Indiana, Maryland, Minnesota, Mississippi, Missouri, New York, North Carolina, Ohio, Pennsylvania, South Carolina, Tennessee, Texas, Virginia, and West Virginia. Co-Editor: *Introduction to Sociology; Selected Readings in Sociology; Introduction to American Government; Readings on the American Way; Analysis of Social Problems.*

Stackpole Series includes: *Contemporary Social Science, Marriage and Family Relations, Dynamic Urban Sociology,* and several others. Home: Lincoln University, Chester County, Pennsylvania (as listed in the publication: *Who's Who In America*).

DR. EVELYN KELSAW BONNER

Dr. Evelyn Kelsaw Bonner is a product of Presbyterian Mission Schools. Born in Alabama, she began her years of education at the Prairie Mission School in Wilcox County, Alabama. Upon graduation from high school at Miller's Ferry in 1959, she enrolled in Mary Holmes College, where she earned an Associate in Arts degree in 1961.

While a student at Mary Holmes, Evelyn worked in the library, painted hallways, scraped and washed windows and sang in the choir. In 1962, Evelyn married David Benjamin Bonner, III, also a product of Presbyterian Mission Schools. The Bonners returned to Mary Holmes College during the summer of 1977 to serve as Volunteers in Mission for six weeks.

Evelyn earned a Bachelor of Arts degree in English from Johnson C. Smith University, Charlotte, North Carolina; a Master of Science degree in Library and Information Services from Atlanta University, Atlanta, Ga.; Post graduate certification in Library Administration Management from the University of Maryland, College Park, Maryland. She has done other course work at the University of Alaska Juneau, and Alaska Pacific University in Anchorage. She is a graduate of the Institute of Cultural Affairs (known as the Ecumenical Institute)- Chicago. She earned a Doctor of Science degree from Nova University, Fort Lauderdale, Florida.

Dr. Bonner recently retired from Sheldon Jackson College in Sitka, Alaska where she and her husband, David, have lived and worked for 27 years. She is a full professor of English and Library and Information Sciences and is Division Chair for Learning Resources.

Evelyn is an elder in the Presbyterian Church. She has served as the 1994 Commencement Speaker at Mary Holmes College and received an Honorary Doctor of Humane Letters degree from Mary Holmes College just prior to the Commencement Address.

Since retirement, Dr. Evelyn Kelsaw Bonner and her husband have worked at Mary Holmes Junior College and are now living in Marshall, Texas, where Dr. Bonner is involved in activities at a local college.

MR. CECIL TIMOTHY ST. CLAIR

Mr. St. Clair was born in Dunedin, Florida. As a high school student, he attended school at Miller's Ferry, where he lived in the dormitory. He earned his high school diploma at Miller's Ferry and received his under graduate degree from Alabama State University. His graduated degree was earned from Wayne State University in Michigan. Further study was done at Catholic University of America, Hampton University and Brown University.

Committed to excellence in the education profession, Cecil's work experience included several teaching and administrative positions with the Detroit Public School District. It was in these positions that Cecil instructed students in mathematics and mentored new teachers in their careers. He also was visiting lecturer at Oakland University in Rochester, Michigan, and taught mathematics at Wayne County Community College. Later Cecil retired as a Program Supervisor for Secondary Mathematics from Detroit Public Schools.

Cecil was a member of numerous professional organizations and honorary societies. Also, he was a member of Alpha Phi Alpha Fraternity.

In addition to having a fulfilling professional career, Cecil was blessed to be married 48 years to Estella St. Clair. Three children were born to this union: Janet, Derrick and Sibyl.

Reflections from a friend:

> Cecil was in fellowship with God.
> A giant as a teacher of math.
> He was willing to help anybody.
> He earned respect by giving respect.

MRS. EVIE MARSHALL HALL

A Success Story by Mrs. Evie Marshall Hall
Miller's Ferry Normal and Industrial High School
Graduation Class of 1930

After 94 glorious and blessed years, it is with humility and thanksgiving that I reflect over the vast experiences, extraordinary influence, many teachers and dynamic leadership of Miller's Ferry Normal and Industrial High School. Students were enrolled from miles around. Some were day students and some were boarders. Included in the enrollment were my three sisters; Willie Mae, Marjorie, Ora Dorothy and I.

The first through twelfth grades, with the exception of second and seventh grades, were spent within the halls and teachings at Miller's Ferry Normal and Industrial High School. Not only the learning, but also the values were instilled in me for me to pass down to others for generations to generations, from my own children to my students. All of this is owed to the grace of God, the instructions and discipline of my parents, and the teaching at Normal and Industrial High School.

A number of persons were integral in my development and growth at the Normal and Industrial High School, especially the teachers. They were wonderful, and they took a keen interest in their work and students. I remember my teachers well. My first grade teacher was Miss Anita Johnson. She was a tall, slim and an exceptional individual. After attending second grade in Birmingham, Alabama, I returned to Miller's Ferry and the next school year I was promoted to the fourth grade. Mrs. Cora Simpson, the principal's wife, taught me fourth and fifth grades. My sixth, eighth and ninth grade teachers respectively were my cousin Miss Rosa Rivers, Miss Bessie Munden and Miss Alphonso Young and Miss Ruth Anderson, a proficient and gifted teacher, and my eleventh and twelfth grades teachers were Professor Benjamin Ridgeway and Professor Auhorn, an African. To make sure we were exposed to the arts and culture, we had classes in Latin and foreign languages. One of our foreign language instructors was Mrs. Massey who taught us French. We were greeted each day with Greek, French or Latin and were required to respond accordingly with the correct reply. We even sang "America" in French in Chapel. Besides the basic school courses we were taught sewing, home economics and music. There were five sewing teachers: Miss Ethel Jackson, Miss Julia Wilson, Mrs. Adell Sanders, Mrs. Fannie Parker, and Mrs. Carey. Mrs. Auhorn was the music teacher and Mrs. Baker taught home economics.

All of my teachers had a big influence on my life. They improved and reinforced what I had been taught at home: respect, good manners and proper behavior. Miller's Ferry Normal and Industrial High School made a difference in my life. My principals while a student at Miller's Ferry Normal and Industrial High School were Rev. Isaac Bonner and Prof. Curtis Simpson. They were professionals and set an example for the student body and the community.

There were 13 of us to graduate in 1930. Miss Fannie Parker was our monitor—the person who helped organize the senior banquet, send invitations, select class colors and motto for the 12th grade that year. My classmates were: Lettie Cook, Lillie Mae Smith, Obie and Alfred Daniels, Jessie Brooks, Eula Wade, Elizabeth Steele, Marzetta Pressley Bethea, and Rhea — who are all deceased; Thelma Pettigrew and Claude Burns, whose whereabouts are unknown; and Dannie Foster Johnson, who lives in Birmingham, Alabama. I currently reside in Pensacola, Florida.

This school prepared me for a lifetime of service and teaching. After completing high school in May 1930, that summer I attended Alabama State University (formerly Alabama State College), a branch in Birmingham, and I received an Associate of Arts degree and a Teachers' Certificate and started teaching in Wilcox County. Miss Bessie Munden, my eighth grade teacher, was the teaching supervisor for the County at that time. I received my Bachelor of Science degree in 1960. Both certificates of diplomas were from Alabama State University. With a commitment and zeal for teaching, I began a lifetime of service to my profession and set an environment for learning for nearly 43 years.

After a rewarding 43 years of teaching, I retired in 1973 but I never retired from a full and active life. I worked with the Senior Citizens of Safford Community Center. I taught proper etiquette, the Sunday School lesson and coordinated programs. For several years, I have written the community news to be published in Selma-Times Journal newspaper. I have been honored and have received a number of certificates of accomplishment for outstanding achievements and service. I was awarded a certificate of achievement as advertiser and news co-coordinator for the Senior Citizens Center; honored by the Retired Senior Volunteer Program for significant service to the community as a senior volunteer; and received a certificate of participation from Tuskegee University Cooperative Extension program Youth Leadership Camp. I am a former Sunday School teacher at Aimwell Baptist Church, Safford, Alabama, former President of the Usher Board, former member of the Senior Choir, President of Young Matrons, and was chairperson of the Program Committee.

Normal and Industrial High School not only prepared me academically, but religiously too. All students were required to take a Bible class. I remember well one particular way we learned about the Bible, and that was from a textbook that contained questions from the Bible. We were required to search the Bible to find the answers to the questions. In addition to school, I attended Sunday School there and learned to love God and our fellow man. All of this was helpful in our knowledge and growth of our spiritual development.

Miller's Ferry Normal and Industrial school was one in a million. The teachers and principal knew the value of mentoring and education. They were interested in the children learning both academically and religiously. They knew the value of encouraging others. I thank this school and my teachers for teaching me responsibility and for teaching us to grow together, to worship together, to serve, to laugh, to cry and to reach out to help others.

Clinton M. Marsh

The following article is about a graduate of Camden Academy. Clinton attended Camden Academy, Knoxville College and Pittsburgh Xenia Seminary, Pittsburgh, Pennsylvania.

Clinton Marsh, a patriarch of the Presbyterian Church (U.S.A.), had one of the most diversified ministries in the denomination. A 1944 graduate of the Pittsburgh-Xenia Seminary, he served in numerous capacities at the national, synod, and presbytery levels.

For eighteen years he was the pastor of the Witherspoon Church in Indianapolis. During those years he was a member of the Board of American Missions in the former United Presbyterian Church of North America, president of the Church Federation of Greater Indianapolis, moderator of the presbytery and synod, and a respected leader in civic and church organizations. Following his years in Indianapolis, he served as area secretary of Evangelism, interim synod executive for the Synod of the South, and associate synod executive for the Synod of Nebraska.

His election as moderator of the General Assembly in 1973 was both preceded and followed by many outstanding contributions. Always an advocate of education, he was a member of the Board of Trustees of Warren Wilson College, Maryville College, and Pittsburgh Seminary. He was a frequent speaker and staunch supporter of New Wilmington Missionary Conference, interim dean of Johnson C. Smith Seminary, and president of Knoxville College.

Clinton Marsh was the organizing secretary of the All-Africa Conference of Churches. He was chosen by the African church leaders to be the administrator of the Ecumenical Program for the Emergency Action in Africa. In this capacity he worked with projects in twenty-eight African countries, helping them to meet their needs as they gained independence.

The Presbyterian Peace Fellowship is on the long and varied list of Clinton's interests. He was moderator for many years and was awarded the title of Moderator Emeritus. He believed that peacemaking was a calling, not a conscience.

The Presbyterian Health, Education, and Welfare Association is on the list because of Clinton Marsh's participation in the Network on Alcohol and Other Drug Abuse. He was devoted to the causes of social justice ministry and spoke and worked to eliminate the destruction caused by the use of alcohol.

During his last years, Marsh was an activist against gun violence. He envisioned and organized Georgians United Against Violence, and he was the driving force behind an anti-gun campaign in Atlanta led by Concerned Black Clergy.

A prolific writer; he contributed frequently to journals and newspapers. He authored *Evangelism Is…*, an examination of the dynamics of the growth and decline of the Presbyterian Church following World War II. Loved and respected nationally and internationally, Clinton's calm and gentle spirit cloaked an unyielding conviction about the causes to which he gave his energy and his life.

- Agnes Marsh

REV. JOHN H. DAVIS

Rev. John H. Davis is a native of Flatwood, Alabama. He received his elementary and junior high education from St. Phillips Lutheran School in Catherine, Alabama in 1938. The following fall John Davis entered high school at Miller's Ferry, but his tenure there was interrupted by his enlistment in the United States Army. At the close of the war he returned home and to school. As a high school student, John was very involved and demonstrated qualities of becoming a leader. John Davis was awarded his high school diploma in 1943 and entered Alabama A & M College at Huntsville, Alabama in the fall of the same year.

John became interested in civil rights in the early forties so he decided to come home from school to his native county, Wilcox, and register to vote. Although he was a veteran, John was not allowed to register.

After earning a B. S. degree from Alabama A & M College in agriculture, Mr. Davis became a successful teacher. He was also involved in the civil rights struggle and candidate for various public offices.

While involved in the civil rights movement, Rev. Davis organized an NAACP (National Association for the Advancement of Colored People) chapter at Alabama A & M College. He worked along with E. D. Nixon and Rev. Martin Luther King, Jr. in the Montgomery Bus Boycott. Rev. Davis ran for Mayor of Ashville, Alabama and served as the delegate at large for the National Democratic Convention that was held in Miami, Florida in 1970. In 1946, Rev. Davis was privileged to hold a 45 minute conference with President Harry Truman to make his plea and to present his Voting Relief Petition many years before the more well-known civil rights struggle began.

For his untiring and dedicated work, Mr. Davis received numerous awards and accolades. The latest significant addition to his honor was becoming a Lutheran minister. He graduated from the Lutheran Concordia Seminary in 1980. Rev. Davis is a retired educator but continues to serve as a minister as well as participate in civic and other activities for the young and elderly.

APPENDIX

WRITTEN REFERENCES

1. Johnson, Sophia Cox, *Beginnings in the Black Belt and Short Stories of the Lives of Dr. Charles Henry and Mrs. Tillie E. Johnson.* Wheaten Printing Company, Birmingham, Alabama, Copyright 1940.

2. Minutes of the Wilcox County Board of Education Meetings

3. Writings on Arlington Literary and Industrial High School by Mrs. Naomi Fisher Hawkins

4. Old records, minutes and programs from Arlington, Miller's Ferry and Prairie Mission Schools

APPENDIX II

Members of the Southern Alabama Teachers
Association

W. J. Edwards,	Snow Hill Ala
John F. Arter,	Annemanie Ala.
Clarence A. Watkey	Snow Hill Ala.
Moe R. Reese,	Millers Ferry Ala.
Lela A. Bennett,	Prairie Ala.
Corinne G. Dansby	Prairie Ala.
Miss Julia L. Jones	Millers Ferry Ala.
E. M. Brown,	Richmond, Ala.
B. A. Ives,	Prairie Ala.
Laura B. Boulden	Anne Manie, Ala.
Mayme E. Greene,	Anne Manie, Ala.
Edward D. Hodgins,	Millers Ferry Ala.
E. A. Hawkins,	Camden Ala.
Thos. M. Elliott	Prairie Ala.
Eliza G. Alden	Anne Manie Ala.
Thomas R. Berry	Millers Ferry Ala.
Lucy Woodward	Annemanie Ala.
Amelia Love	Prairie, Ala.
B. Lela Stephens	Prairie, Ala.
Robert Micheal.	Anne Manie, Ala.
N. J. Holley.	Millers Ferry, Ala.
W. J. Wilson,	Camden, Ala.
Josephine Wilson	" "

Ira U. Howson	Camden Ala.
Lula P. Wilkerson	Camden Ala.
Annie K Wilson	Camden Ala.
Eva L. Williams	Canton Bend, Ala.
L. P. Williams	Camden, Ala.
Willa E. Hight	Miller's Ferry Ala.
R. H. Wilmer	" " "
C. H. Johnson	" " "
Miss S.D. Johnson	" " "
" J. B. Dick	" " "
" L. E. Williams	" " "

Mr. N. B. Cotton	Canton Bend. Ala.
Mrs. J. N. Cotton	Prairie. Ala.
Mrs. Ella Cotton	Canton Bend. Ala.
Mrs. M. L. Hight	Camden, Ala.

268   School Roll.

Beginning
Oct. 12 - '09.   Fall and Winter terms '09 - '10 —

1 Maggie Lee White		1 00
2 Carrie Southall		1 00
3 Irene Southall		1 00
4 Nellie Southall		50
5 Earnest Southall		50
6 Edna Arter		50
7 Ruth Arter		50
8 Ralph Arter		00
9 Lizzie Kimbro		2 00
10 Mary Hamilton		1 00
11 Thurman Hope		50
12 Mattie Bridges		50
13 Sadie Lewis		50
14 Emma Dumas		1 00
15 Mamie Davenport		x 50
16 Albert Griffin		50
17 Lucile Griffin		50
18 Rosa Fisher		50
19 Abram Fisher		50
20 Corrie Lassiter		5.
21 Nettie Belle Lassiter		5.
22 Mary Duncan		2.
23 Willie Duncan		2.
24 Marie Threadgill		5.
25 Gertrude Threadgill		5.
26 Louise Marsh		5.
27 Lonnie Lynch	work	5.
28 Percy Dumas		5
29 Marguerite Nelson		5
30 Dora Marshall		2 .
		5

#	Name			Amount
35	Lucy Michael			50
36	Tillie Brazelton			50
37	Cherry Fisher			50
38	George Marsh			50
39	James Bridges			264
40	Ellen Ann Curtis			50
41	Willie Taylor			50
42	Mamie Taylor			50
43	Floyd Matthews			50
44	Rosetta Pernell			1.00
45	Salie Pernell due 45¢			55
46	Willie Ann Kimbro			40
47	Kennedy			100
48	Lola Auburn			50
49	Riggs			
50	Riggs			
51				
52	Willie Brown			40
53	Emma Hudson } Book			100
54	Henry Hudson }			50
55	Emma Purnell			100
56	Mary Purnell			100
57	Minnie Purnell			50
58	Caroline Dumas			50
59	Isaac Bridges (Work)			100
60	Lillie Robinson			100
61	Sadie Michael			50
62	Robert Michael			50
63	Eddie Dumas			50
64	Essie Kimbro			45
65	Joseph Fisher			50
66	Emma L Fisher			50
67	John T. Bridges			50
68	Mary Matthews			

Camden Ala. Nov. 6-8 '07

The Southern Alabama Teachers'
Association Met At Camden Academy
Nov. 6, 1907. Devotions were led by Prof.
J. N. Cotton. No. 281 was sung. 101st Ps.
was read No. 1 was sung. Prayer
was offered by several.

On motion the presidents
address was post poned until Thursday
evening.

Enrollment of delegates.
There were 18 enrolled with an
enrollment fee amounting to $4.75
Miscellaneous business was called
for. On request Rev. Arter gave
in a few words, the History of the
Association.

On motion it was decided
that a committee on entertainment
be appointed. Rev. Arter, Prof Walker,
Prof. J. N. Cotton, constituted the
Committee. By common consent it was
decided that a committee on the press
Educational Status of the Negro be appo-
ted. The following were appointed,
Rev. B. A. Sines
Mrs. R. P. Williams
Miss Bennett
Miss Woodward
Prof. Walker
Prof. Berry
Rev. N. G. Nilson

An address "The Ideal Teacher" by Rev. Arter, of Anniston Ala. The address was very instructive. Some of the thoughts suggested, "Our Savior was held up as The "Ideal Teacher" Teachers must know things; must work for the good he can do, not for place Read school journals, The Bible should be read, prayer fully." The subject was discussed by Rev. B. A. Imes, He said a teacher in order to be successful must put heart into the work. must love those whom he teaches. The work of a teacher requires a very high standard of Christian character."

On motion the association adjourned to meet again — 9.00 A. M. Thursday morning
Rev. W. G. Nilson Pre
Mrs. P. S. Stephens — Sec

Course of Study

Of The Arlington Literary and Industrial School

From October 15th 1912 – Rev. J. T. Arter, A.B., B.D., Principal; Rev. G. G. Daniel, D.D., M. Pd., Dean.

Primary Department

First Year

Fall Term	Winter Term	Spring Term
Reading – Wall Print – Primer – Phonics	Reading – The Primer – Phonics – Oral Spelling	Reading – Completing the Primer – Oral Spelling – Phonics
Number Work – Counting to 20 – Multiplication Tables – Writing Numbers.	Number – Counting to 100 Mult-Tables – Writing the numbers.	Number – Simple addition and Subtraction of not more than 3 figures.
Writing – Forming letters on "o" basis; – hooks – joining strokes	Writing – Small and Cap. letters – joining letters	Writing – Transcription from Primer
Story telling – Repeating the story	Story - telling	Story - telling
Form &c Lessons on form size, color, weight measures.	Form &c	Form &c
Paper – folding	Paper – folding	Paper – folding – Making Envelopes
Sewing (for girls) Needle and Thimble drill – stitches with red	Sewing (for girls) Seaming, running, felling, hemming – the back stitch.	Sewing (for girls) Herring bone feather – stitch hat ting.

Course of Study, Cont⁰

(Primary Dept)

Fall Term, Cont'd	Winter Term, Cont'd	Spring term, cont'd
and blue thread on white cloth — the lockstitch		Action Songs — Poetry
Action Songs — Nursery Rhymes — Bible Stories	Action Songs — Poetry for little folk — Bible Stories	Bible Stories
Manners and Morals — Innocence, gentleness, tenderness, trustfulness, friendliness	Manners and Morals	Manners and Morals

Second Year

Fall Term	Winter Term	Spring Term
Reading — First Reader Inflection — Pause — Tone — Oral Spelling	Reading — First Reader — Oral Spelling	Reading — Completing First Reader Oral Spelling.
Arithmetic Notation & Numeration to 5 figures — Mult. Tables — Addition & Subtraction to 5 figures — mental Arithmetic	Arithmetic — Notation and Numeration Mult. Tables Addition + Subtraction — mental Arithmetic	Arithmetic — Tots — Mental Arith Not. + Numeration Review Roman Notation
Writing — Transcription and Dictation from Reader.	Writing — Transcription and Dictation	Writing — To write from Dictation any selection from Reader
Story telling	Story telling	Story telling

Course of Study, Cont.
Elementary Department
Second Year

Fall Term	Winter Term	Spring Term
Reading — A Fourth Reader — Oral Spelling	Reading — Fourth Reader — Oral Spelling	Reading — Fourth Reader Complete — Oral Spelling.
Arithmetic — Prime factors — H.C.F., L.C.M. Common Fractions	Arithmetic — Common Fractions	Arithmetic — Common fractions cont.
Writing — Spencerian Copy Bk no 2 — Transcription + Dictation — Test Words —	Writing — Copy Book no 2. Transcription + Dictation	Writing — Spencerian Copy book no 2. — Transcription and Dictation
Geography — North America	Geography — North America and United States	Geography — United States
Grammar — Maxwell's Pt I Sentence making	Grammar — Classification of sentences (Maxwell, Pt I)	Grammar — Division of Grammar — noun inflection
Historical Stories	Historical stories	Historical Stories
Manual Training — Household articles	Manual Training — Household articles	Manual Training Household articles
Elementary Physiology	Elementary Physiology	Elementary Physiology
Nature Study — Kitchen gardening + Flowers	Nature Study — Kitchen gardening and Flowers	Nature Study — Kitchen garden + Flowers
Drawing — From Copy — Shading	Drawing — From Copy Shading	Drawing From Copy + shading
Sewing — Basting and Felling Dressmaking — Embroidery	Sewing — Dress making — Embroidery — Lace	Sewing — Dressmaking Embroidery Laces
Vocal Music — The Staff Major Scales	Vocal Music — Key Signatures — Solfa	Vocal Music — Solfa
Bible History — Old Test.	Bible History — Old Test.	Bible History — Old Test.
Manners + Morals	Manners and Morals	Manners + Morals

Course of study, cont°
Elementary Department
Second Year

Fall Term	Winter Term	Spring Term
Reading — A Fourth Reader — Oral Spelling	Reading — Fourth Reader — Oral Spelling	Reading — Fourth Reader Complete — Oral Spelling.
Arithmetic — Prime factors — H.C.F., L.C.M. Common Fractions	Arithmetic — Common Fractions	Arithmetic — Common fractions cont°
Writing — Spencerian Copy Bk no 2 — Transcription & Dictation — Test Words —	Writing — Copy Book no 2. Transcription & Dictation	Writing — Spencerian Copy book no 2. — Transcription and Dictation
Geography — North America	Geography — North America and United States	Geography — United States
Grammar — Maxwell's Pt I Sentence making	Grammar — Classification of sentences (Maxwell, Pt I)	Grammar — Division of Grammar — noun inflection
Historical Stories	Historical stories	Historical Stories
Manual Training — Household articles	Manual Training — Household articles	Manual Training Household articles
Elementary Physiology	Elementary Physiology	Elementary Physiology
Nature Study — Kitchen gardening & Flowers	Nature Study — Kitchen gardening and Flowers	Nature Study — Kitchen garden & Flowers
Drawing — From Copy — Shading	Drawing — From Copy Shading	Drawing — From Copy & shading
Sewing — Basting and Fitting Dressmaking — Embroidery	Sewing — Dressmaking — Embroidery — Lace	Sewing — Dressmaking Embroidery Laces
Vocal Music — The Staff Major Scales	Vocal Music — Key Signatures — Solfa	Vocal Music — Solfa
Bible History — Old Test.	Bible History — Old Test.	Bible History — Old Test.
Manners & Morals	Manners and Morals	Manners & Morals

Course of Study, Cont°

(Primary Dept) Third Year.

Fall Term.	Winter Term.	Spring Term.
Reading — A Secon Reader Pause — Emphasis, Tone — Oral Spelling	Reading — Secon Reader Oral Spelling	Reading — Completing Reader — Oral Spellg
Arithmetic — Notation and numeration to millions — Short Multiplication Short Division — Multiplication & Division Table — Mental Arithmetic.	Arithmetic — Short Multiplication & Short Division — Mental Arithmetic	Arithmetic — Long Multiplication and Division by factors — Casting out 9's — Mental Arithmetic.
Writing — Transcription and Dictation	Writing — Transcription and Dictation	Writing — Transcription and Dictation
Story telling	Story telling	Story Stelling
Geography — A talk about the earth	Geography — A talk about the earth.	Geography — Talk about Alabama
Drawing — Outlines	Drawing — Outlines	Drawing — Outlines
Nature Study — Plants	Nature Study — Plants	Nature Study — Plants
Manual Training — Rule — Compasses & Try Square — Saw and jack plane	Manual Training — Rule Compasses, Try Sq. — Saw & Jack plane	Manual Training — Rule Compasses, Try Sq., Saw & Jack Plane.
Music — Rote Singing	Music — Rote Singing Bible St: N. Test.	Music — Rote Singing Bible Stories — N. T.

Course of Study, Cont.

(Primary Dept.) Third Year.

Fall Term.	Winter Term.	Spring Term.
Reading — A Secon Reader Pause — Emphasis, Tone — Oral Spelling	Reading — Secon Reader Oral Spelling	Reading — Completing Reader — Oral Spellg
Arithmetic — Notation and Numeration to millions — Short Multiplication — Short Division — Multiplication & Division Tables — Mental Arithmetic.	Arithmetic — Short Multiplication & Short Division — Mental Arithmetic	Arithmetic — Long Multiplication and Division by factors — Casting out 9's — Mental Arithmetic.
Writing — Transcription and Dictation	Writing — Transcription and Dictation	Writing — Transcription and Dictation
Story telling	Story telling	Story Stelling
Geography — A talk about the earth	Geography — A talk about the earth.	Geography — Talk about Alabama
Drawing — Outlines	Drawing — Outlines	Drawing — Outlines
Nature Study — Plants	Nature Study — Plants	Nature Study — Plants
Manual Training — Rule — Compasses & Try Square — Saw an Jack plane	Manual Training — Rule — Compasses, Try Sq. — Saw & Jack plane	Manual Training — Rule Compasses, Try Sq., Saw & Jack Plane.
Music — Rote Singing	Music — Rote Singing	Music — Rote Singing
Bible Stories — N. Test.	Bible Stories — N. Test.	Bible Stories — N. T.
Manners and Morals	Manners and Morals	Manners & Morals

3

Tuition Summer 1912

15	Flossie Mathews	.25 —	✓
"	Floyd Mathews	.25 —	✓
"	Rebecca Mason	.25 —	✓
"	~~Jenkins~~ Pigson	25 —	✓
"	Clarence Robinson	25	✓
"	Caroline Dumas	25	✓
"	Rosa Gregory	25	✓
16	Maggie Lee White	25 —	✓
"	Pearl Duncan	26	✓
	Mauetta Mathews	25	✓
	Susie Mathews	26	✓
	B. R. Skinner	25	✓
	Rosetta Purnell	25	✓
	Lillie Bridges	25	✓
	Dasie Fisher	25	✓
	Adonia Dunham	25 —	✓
	Neda Fisher	25	✓
	Cecelia Frazier	26	✓
	Albert Griffin Jr.	25	✓
	Mamie Threadgill	25	✓
	Gertie Threadgill	25	✓
	Enoch Hall	25	✓
	Ethel Hall	25	✓
	Minnie Purnell	25	✓
	Mary Purnell	25	✓
	Emaline Purnell	25	✓
	Leslie Robinson	25	✓
	Mamie Davenport	25	✓
	S Evana Kimbrough	25	
	Frank Kimbrough	25	
	Isaac Bridges	25	
	John T. Bridges	25	
	Eva Cook	25 —	

Record 1901 and 1902, From Sept. to May,

1 bbl clothing L. M. S Washburn Ill.
1 " " Junior Union Fair Iowa.
1 " " W. M. S Hamilton Ohio.
1 " " Mrs Anna Bollman & Mrs David Hornock
    Homestead Congregation Orion Ill.
Miss M. Jean Hourson & mother Franks Ill
    Sonwick congregation Reading Room   10.00
1 bbl & 1 box clothing East Palestine Ohio.
3 bbls of clothing Harrisville Pa Harmony
   Congregation.
1 bbl of clothing W. M. S. Caledonia N. Y.
1 " " " York N. Y. Miss. Soc.
1 " " " Hanover Sdg. Cong.
1 box of shoes Martins Ferry Ohio
    E. C. Boyd.
1 bbl of Christmas Goods 1st U. P. Church Ladies aid
Allegheny Pa, Ladies Home Mission Society
   Posted to 12/9/1901.
2 bbls. Cedarville Ohio L. M. S.
2 " north Bend Neb L. M. S

Price List,

Apples (evaporated)	.08 cts. per lb.	
Apples (canned)	.08⅓ " per can	
Bacon ~~Table~~ 2 7½	~~11½ cents~~	
Bakingpowder 15 ~~67½~~	" per lb.	
Bulk meat	18 cents	
Beans Lima	.06¢ per lb.	
Beans Navy	.08⅓ " "	
Beef (Roast)	08¢ ": 67½"	
" Steak	10¢ " "	
Beef (canned roast)	~~77~~ 67½	
Beef Tongue	1.87½ x per can	
Beef tripe (canned)	13 ¢	
Butter (country)	20¢ per lb 2	
Butter creamery	37½¢ " "	
Cheese	16¢	
Eggs per Doz.	20 ~~26¢~~ 32½	
Grits per lb.	.02¢	
Hams " "	15	
~~Lard~~	~~0~~ .09	
Flour	03¢	
Rye	10¢	
Meal	65	
Condensed milk	.07½¢	
Rolled Oats	10¢	
Coffee	~~#~~ 15 ¢	
Tea	20¢	
Soap (Lenox)	.03¼¢	
Soap Ivory	04¢	
Soap Chipped	.05½¢ per lb	
Bleech	.04½¢ " "	
Bluing	.04¢	
Rice	5½ .06¢ per lb	
Prunes	.08¢ per lb.	

Sugar	.05¼¢ per lb.
Brooms	18¾
Dusters	.08¢ each
Salmon	~~15½~~ 11
Tomatoes	.07½ per can
Lamp chimneys	.05¢
O.D.C.	5½ ~~2¢~~ per lb
Pearline	.03¢
Syrup	26¢ per gall.
Salt	.0¾ " lb.
Vinegar	18¢ per gall.
Yeast	.03⅓ " box
Sweet Potatoes	75¢ per Bu.
Apple Butter	07½¢ " lb.
Mackerel	.07½ each
Cans Rib Roast	10½¢ lb.
Cans Sausage	12½ per can
Pepper	12½
Fish	12½
Macaroni	.06½ lb.
Canned Corn	.08 can
Salt	.00¾ lb.
Corn	.08 can
Cabbage	~~.02¼~~ .02
Beef Rib (c	10½
Onions	35¢ Gal
Irish Pot	85 bus
Vanilla	2.50 qt.
Soda	7½ lb.
Jelly (can or gal	.08 per jar
Nutmeg	7½ per Doz.
Mustard	.08
Pickles (Sweet	.07½
" (Sour)	19

Bills reported for March 1916

	Boarding	Farm	Shops	Tuition	Dom. Science	Sa...
C. & E. Lamar Selma Ala Mar 23rd 1916						
Sack Phosfe		16 50 — # 16 50				
0 sacks Cotton seed meal		31 00 · 31 00				
Drayage			80	Total # 48 30		
Dallas Lumber Co. Manufacturing Co.						
Selma Ala Feb. 29th 1916						
S/R			128 24			
21 B/R			2 75 — # 130 99			
8 By check	30 00					
20 " "	25 00			53 00	Dues 75 99	
The McClure Co. Saginaw Mich. Mar. 10-1916				75 24		
Note and Int.						
Tissier Hardware Co. Mar 9th 1916 Selma Ala						
6 4" Terra Cotta Ys.		35	2 10			
6 4" " " Elbows		25	1 50			
20 Pcs 4" Terra Cotta Pope 40 07			2 80	Total # 6 40		
Tissier Hardware Co. Selma Mar 9th 1916						
1 Set Breeching			# 5 50			
2 Back Bands		1 50	3 00			
2 Belly "		1 00	2 00			
2 Ventiplex Pads		75	1 50			
2 pair 7-1-0 Traces		1 00	2 00			
8 1" Hame Strings			1 25			
2 Collars		4 00	8 00			
2 Yoke Strings		75	1 50			
½ doz. ½" open eye bolt Snap			38			
1 pair Dbl. Breast Chains			50			
1 ball Shoe Thread			10			
1 Sewing Awl & Handle			25			
1 dz 1-¼ Snaps			60			
pair 550 Brass Ball Top Hames			2 50			
2 " #2 Trace Pipes			4 00	Total # 33 68		

Bills reported Dec. 29th for Dec. 1915.

	Boarding	Farm	Shops	Tuition	Dom. Science	Salarie

ttanooga Roofing & Foundry Company Dec. 3rd 1915. Chattanooga
6" Single Beaded lap joint E. T.
Outside Mitres
-4" Galv. Condr pipe Freight Bill reported for $
ross 6" Wire hangers $32 66
nly 4" Galv. Condr. pipe Ells
-5" Single Beaded lap joint E T
- Outside Mitres
-3" Galv. Condr pipe
-3" Galv. Condr pipe Ells
Gross 5" Wire hangers Total amount $79 97

bbins Hardware Company Dec 14 - 1915-
w butts 3½ × 3½ 12½ - - - 38
nob Locks 22½ - - - 67
cks Cement 2 bbls 2 40 4 80
3bl Lime 85 85
ft 35 × 2 Netting 2 03 60
Netgingstaple 15 07
8 finishing Nail
6d Nails 30# 03 90
eg 8d Cem Nails 2 45 2 45
eg 16d Cem Nails 2 40 Total $13 12

bbins Hardware Company Dec 22nd 1915-
Key fitted to lock 15
Spark plug 1 00 Total $1 15

Byrd and Company Dec 1st 1915-
Bale Broom Corn 238 @ 8½¢ $24 40

.C. Adler and Company Nov. 29 1915-
Mattress $4 00

Total amount for Dec. $2
$122 64

ACCOUNT NO._____   SHEET NO._____

NAME   *Geraldine Tyson,*

ADDRESS   *J. E. Tyson 209½ # N. Cedar St Mobile*

TERMS.
RATING.
CREDIT LIMIT.

DATE	ITEMS	Folio	√	DEBITS	DATE	ITEMS	Folio	√	CREDITS
Entered 1917									
Aug 8	to Sept. 8th board			6 00	Aug 9	Cash on board			$ 18 00
" "	" washing			1 00	" "	Cash on washing			3 00
Sept 8	to Oct. 8 board			6 00					
" "	washing			1 00					
Oct " 8	to Nov. 5th board			6 00					$ 21 00
" "	" " " washing			1 00					
				21 00					
Oct. 5	tablet & peanuts			10	Oct. 25	Cash			$ 15 00
Nov. 5	to Soap & starch for				Nov. 5	Cash			10 00
	Aug, Sept Oct & Nov.			48					
Nov. 5	to Jan 29th board			18 00		Bal. due			81
" "	" " " washing			3 00					
	Music			3 75					
	Soap & starch for Nov.								
	Dec, & Jan.			48					$ 25 81
				$ 25 81					
Jan 29	to balance			81	Dec. 1	Cash			81
Jan 29	to Feb. 26th board			6 00		Cash			$ 20 00
Feb 26	to March 26 "			6 00		Cash from shoes			3 50
Mar 26	to Apr. 23 "			6 00					23 50
	3 months washing			3 00					
	3 month music			3 75					
				$ 24 75					
	Soap & starch 3 months			36					25 11
				$ 25 11					
						Transfered			

TERMS.

RATING. Mr. U. S. Thompson   NAME Eddie Thompson
CREDIT LIMIT.   ADDRESS Ellaville, Ga.

1917

DATE	ITEMS	Folio	√	DEBITS	DATE	ITEMS	Folio	√	CREDITS
Sept 11	Entrance fee			2 00					
" "	to Oct. 9th board			6 00					
" "	" " " washing			1 12	Sept 11	Cash			$9 87
	Hauling trunk			25					
	Breaking basket			1 00					
Oct 8	Board from Oct 9th				" 8				
	to Nov. 6			6 50					
	Washing			1 12					
				$8 62	Oct 8	Money Order			8 00
Nov. 6	to Dec. 4th board			6 50		Bal due			62
" "	" " " washing			1 12	Nov. 3	Cash			9 00
				$7 62	" 7	"			3 8
Oct 9	Cash			3 8					
Nov. 5	" "			1 38					
	To bal due			62					$9 38
				$9 40					
Dec. 4	to Jan 1st board			6 50					
" 12	" " wash			1 12	Dec. 8	By Cash			$7 62
Nov 12	Eddie Thompson			2 00	"	"			15
	Rally 200 Laund & postage 50¢			50		Bal due			2 35
				$10 12					10 12
Jan 1	to Jan 24th			6 50	Jan 7	Cash			$7 62
" "	" " " washing			1 12		Bal due			2 35
	Bal due			2 35					$9 97
				$9 97					
	Bal due			2 35					$7 62
Jan 29	to Feb 26 board			3 62	Feb	Cash			

TERMS.

RATING. Mrs. Ella L. ~~Thomas~~ Browning

CREDIT LIMIT.

NAME Alice Glenn

ADDRESS 420 N. Devilliere St. Pensacola

DATE	ITEMS	Folio	v	DEBITS	DATE	ITEMS	Folio	v	CREDITS
Oct. 4	Entrance fee			2 00	Oct. 4	By cash			$2 00
"	to Nov. 1st board			6 50	Nov. 1	Cash			6 00
"	Laundry fee			50					
Nov. 1	to Nov 29 board			6 50	Nov. 1	Cash			6 00
Nov 29	to Dec. 27 "			6 00	Dec. 1	Cash			6 00
				$23 00		Balance			10 00
									$23 00
Nov 27	to Balance			10 00	Nov	By washing			1 75
Dec 27	to Jan 24 board			6 50	"	" ironing			18
Jan 24	to Feb 4 "			2 75	Dec	Miss Stone & Eddie			2 00
	Transportation			1 25		Miss Stone			35
					Jan	Eddie Thompson			25
	$2.25			$20 50					$4 93
									12 07
									$12 00
Feb 11	to Balance			$17 07	Feb 11	By cash			$15 00
					Feb 11	Balance due			2 07
									$17 07

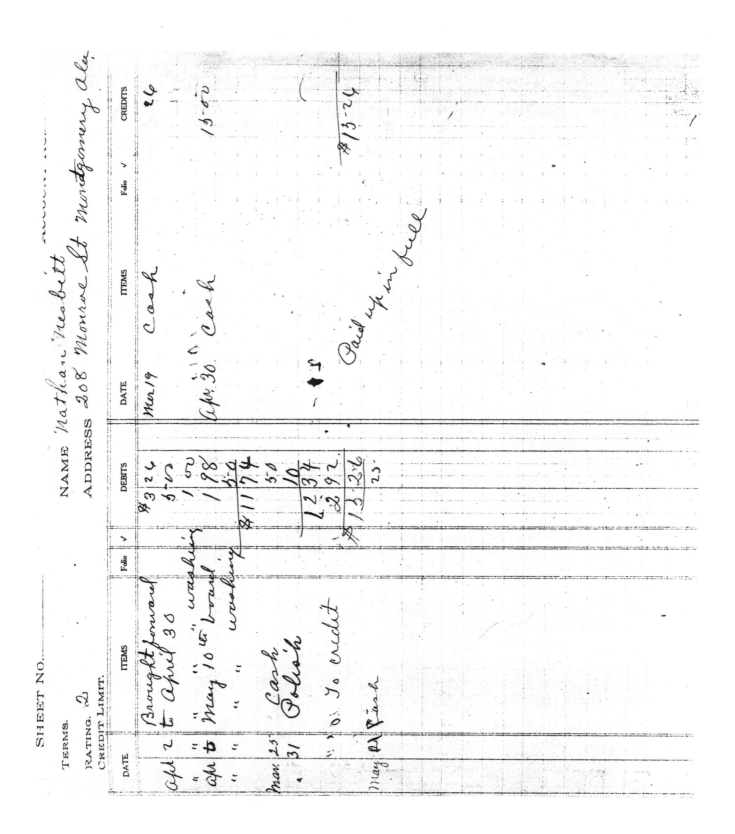

TERMS.
RATING.
CREDIT LIMIT.

NAME William Marianna Harrison Nellie Ruth Harrison

ADDRESS Homewood, 84 N. Pittsburgh Pa
Mrs Ella Harrison

DATE	ITEMS	Folio	V	DEBITS		DATE	ITEMS	Folio	V	CREDITS
Sept 10	Entrance fee			2 00		Sept 10	Cash on hand			6 5 0
"	to Oct 8 1st panel			6 50		"	Entrance fee			2 00
"	Arithmetic			65		"				
	Pencil & Tablet			06						
	Composition boxes			16						
	Tablet			05						
	stylet & pencil									
Oct 8	to Nov 5 2nd panel			6 50		Oct 27	Cash			7 00
	Laundry fee			50		" 31	Cash			7 00
Nov 5	to Dec 3			6 50			Bal. due			46
	" "			6 50						$22 96
				22 96						
Nov 5	To bal.			46		Nov 14	Cash			46
1918						1918				
Jan 1	Board from Dec 3			1 50		Jan 1	By Cash			1 50
	to Feb 31			2 50		Jan 1	" Cash			3 50
Jan 1	to Jan 29 2nd panel					Jun 18	" Cash			3 50
Jan 29	to Feb 26 3rd panel			50		Feb 2	Cash			2 60
Feb 26	to March 26			6 50		Mar 3	Cash			6 50
Feb 26	to March 26			6 50						6 50
Mar 26	to Apr. 23 3rd panel			6 50		Mar 22	By cash			6 50

TERMS.

NAME Johnny Mae Jones

RATING. Mrs Louie Jackson ADDRESS Buena Vista Ga,

CREDIT LIMIT.

DATE	ITEMS	Folio	✓	DEBITS		DATE	ITEMS	Folio	✓	CREDITS	
Sept 11	Entrance fee			2	00	Sept 11	Cash			2	00
"	to Oct. 9 to travel			6 6 0		"	"			6 6 0	
	Hauling trunk			25							
	Bal. due from last year laund.			2 3 6		Oct. 11	Cash			3 00	
	Laund fee for Sept			4 0		Sept	By washing			4 20	
	Stamps			2 2			Cash			03	
	Stamps			06		Nov	Cash			3 5 0	
Oct. 9	to Rec. to travel			6 5 0		Oct. wash Miss Steve				1 00	
Nov 6	to Rec. Oct "			6 5 0			Mrs Hawkins			1 00	
							" Thompson			1 00	
							Eddie Thompson			1 00	
							Nathan Nesbitt				
	To credit			$16 0 9						$17 23	
					1 84						
				$17 23							
						Dec 6 to Credit				$1 14	

268

Report of Culinary Department
Feb. 6, 1912,
Breakfast Cooks,
Mamie Etheridge, Amanda Grayson,

Waitresses
Olga Nichols, Willie Nichols,
Tempie Gildersleeve, Carrie Moore,

Dish washers
Ida Henderson, Amanda McDonal.
Dortha Marshall, Minnie Oldham,

Industrial Girls
Cammie Lee Smith, Mary Purnell,
Mattie Dumas, Viola Dickenson,

Supper Cooks,
Daisy Kennedy,
Shelly Starks

"   .'   .. Feb. 7, 1912

Breakfast Cooks
Amanda Grayson,
Mamie Etheridge

Waitresses
Olga Nichols, Willie Nichols
Tempie Gildersleeve, Carrie Moore,

"
Dish was here
Ida Henderson, Bertha Powell
Amanda Holmes, Dortha Marshall,
Minnie Oldham, Ruth Ray,
Viola Davis, Eva Webb,

Industrial Girls
Ida Henderson, Bertha Powell
Dortha Marshall, Gertrude Henderson
Supper Cook
Dortha Marshall
Gertrude Henderson,

"Farm Department"

1	Sets Wagon Gear	2	Two-horse farm wagons
8	" Plow "	6	Two " plows
6	New Collars	1	one horse spring wagon
3	Prs. Stretchers	5	One " "
6	Sets Double Trees	4	Kentucky pony turning plows
3	Drag Scraper	8	Scuter stocks
22	Turning plow points	6	Planter Jr. Cultivators
38	Sweeps	6	Spring Tooth Harrows
1	Sub-soil Plow	4	Side Harrows
1	Ensilage Cutter	1	2 horse section harrow
1	Silo	1	Disk Harrow
6	Mules	2	Corn Planters
1	Horse	1	Mowing Machine
38	Head of Hogs	1	Hay Rake
38	Head of Cattle	2	Fertilize Distributer
	Wood Saw	1	Cotton planter
1	Gasoline Engine	1	Cane Mill and Evaporator
1	One Horse Wagon	(	Cotton Planter)
		1	Feed Grinding Mill
		1	Pea Huller
		16	Feeding Hogs

1906 Domestic Science Table

Boarders.
Domestic Science opened Nov. 13. 1906
Charges .08 per meal

Mrs. Micheal
Dinner

Nov 13	" "	.08
" 14	" "	.08
" 15	" "	.08
" 16	" "	.08
" 19	" "	.08
" 20	" "	.08
" 21	" "	.08
" 22		.08
" 23	Paid in full	.08
Nov 26	" "	.08
" 27	" "	.08
" 28	" "	.06
Dec 3	" "	.06
" 4	" "	.06
" 5	" "	.06
" 6	" "	.06
" 7	" "	.06
" 10	" "	.06
" 11	" "	.06
" 12	" "	.06
" 13	" "	.06
" 14	" "	.06
" 17	" "	.06
" 18	" "	.06
" 20	" "	.06
" 21		.06

Paid in full

"Saw Mill"

1 B'ld'g 40 X 75 feet.
Lbr. including 800 feet in Vamps, Kilns etc 28000 ft.
Shingles = 1800

X 2 Saw Mill Machinery as follows (Complete)
1 - 40 H.P. Engine   1 12" x 48" Solid
1 - 50 H.P. Boiler   1 Set 10 Bevel Gearing
1 Saw Husk Complete   1 1 15/16 x 40 ft. Shafting with pulley
1 Carriage 12 ft.   1 6" x 28" Steel Split
1 Butt or Cut off Saw   38 ft. 6" Belting (Rubber)
      Complete.   26 " 4"   "   "
1 DeLoach - 3 saw Edger   35 " 12"   "   "
1 American   42 " 8"   "   "
      4 Saw Lath Machine   40 " 10"   "   "
1 Boss Shingle Machine   22 " 6"   "   "
4 Hustler Planing Machine   72 " 12"   "   "
1 200 ft. Dust Conveyor   56 " 8"   "   Leather
1 Pump 3 x 6   78 " 8"   "   "
4 Lbr. Dollees   28 " 4"   "   "
1 Shingle Packing Mach.   46 " 6"   "   Howdy
2 Extra 5 4" Diston   54 " 4"   "   Leather
   Inserted Tooth Saw.   2 Log Wagon 5" Complete
1 2" Counter Shaft   With Chains & Hooks
   Equipped with Culies   2 4" Go Devils
3 12 X 36' solid   1 Extra set Dust Grates
1 8" X 28" solid   8 Peories
2 8" x 52" Steel Split   6 "   Handles
1 10" x 28"   "   4 CC saw "
2 6" x 48"   "   3 "   "   "

98 – 99

Inventory — "Kitchen" — May 27, 1918

1	Range — Double	2	Colanders
1	Bread Oven — 80 loaf	2	Gallon Cup
9	Food and Water Boilers	3	Wooden Spoons
7	Large Stew Pans	6	Large Tin Pans
1	Meat Board	2	Draining Spoon
1	Sifter (Piece)	2	Wire Spoon
2	Rolling Pins	4	Cake Turners
1	Bread Mallet	1	Egg Whisp
1	Biscuit Cutter	3	Grater
1	Large Coffee Boiler	2	Potato Masher
6	Coffee Pots	10	Large Bread Pans
6	Skillets	30	Small " "
2	Dust Pan	9	Dish Pans
2	Shovel	1	Muffin Pan
1	Cupboard	2	Small Enamel Kettles
1	Safe	5	Lard Cans
4	Mop	1	Water Tub
7	~~Meat Board~~	1	Bread Tub
2	Lamp	2	Wash Pans
2	Stove Cleavers	2	Wash Boards
2	Sausage Mill	20	Pie Pans
2	Can opener (Piece)	3	Round Enamel Pans
2	Dipper	1	Round tin Pan
6	Paring Knives	6	Wooden Tubs
6	Extra Tops	4	Tables
2	Scales	4	Sinks
		4	Water Buckets

Dining Room

144	Chairs	12	Cream Pitchers
10	Tables	18	...

Up to May 15th 1916.

Truck Farming · Year 1916.

Garden no 1.

			$	¢
bv.	"	Fertilizer & Seed for tomato bed	3	00
"	"	Seed Potato	10	00
"	"	Garden Seed	11	00
"	"	Chuffers	4	25
"	"	Seed Peanuts	6	00
"	"	Sun flower Seed	1	00
"	"	Caffa Corn		50
"	"	Cover Peanut house	2	00
Preparing Peanut land			6	00
"	Sweet Potato land		8	00
"	Dynamite Cut		6	00
"	Garden no 2 Preparation		8	00
Thompson Spring cut preparing			10	00
Planting beans patch			2	00
" Watermelon patch			10	00
" Irish potato "			16	00
" Preperation & planting Garden No. 3.			7	00
" & Tomato patch no 1			10	00
" " " no. 2			8	00
Fertilize for Truck Gardens			60	00
Smith cut, potatoes Fertilize & labor			7	00
Cook cut - millet planting & prep. land			4	00
Beck house truck, Labor up to may 15th			12	00
Deep Well cut. Preparing land & sowing millet			6	00
Barn cut - Okery preparation			3	00
ay 10	Labor, 6 hands (2 men @ .75 per h & 2 women @ .50 ende)		4	00
10 "	2 men fixing fence (75 per day each)		1	50
11	girls & 3 boys labor		4	25
11	1 mule also may 10th @ 50¢ per day.		1	00
12	" " and			
13				

3 8 Chisel saw bits

1 1 pt. Detroit Lubricator

1 Flue Expander

    Inventory

6 doz. Irons

36 Wash boards

16 Ironing Boards

~~24~~ ~~Boilers~~

1 3/4 Pew Ejector

    Lubricator

Laundry

~~4 Stoves~~

3 tables

1 kettle

3 Stoves

1 ~~Hot water heater~~

Domestic Science

2 Stoves

2 Muffin Tins

6 pans

1 Baker

1 Skillet

2 Large Spoons

1/2 doz. Table "

1 doz. Tea "

1 " Knives and Forks

1 doz. Plates

1 doz. Dessert Plates

1 dz. Breakfast Bowls

1 doz. Chairs

3 Sets Curtains

3 Shades

1 doz. Napkins

1 Silence Cloth

1 Table Cover

4 Tables

Water Plant

1 Pump

1 Tank

3 Bath Rooms, tubs lavatories & Closets Complete

2 Hall Floor Sinks

3 hot water tanks

4 Kitchen Sinks

24 laundry stationary tubs

1 air food

800 feet of vitrit. Clay pipe

1 Engine

"Blacksmith Shop"

2	Anvils	3	Stock
2	Foot Edge	6	Wood Rasps
3	Drawing Knife	4	Vice
3	Brace	72	Drills
1	Hack Saw (Broken)	18	Dies
2	Steel Square	4	Hardies
4	Screw Driver	6	Flatters
4	Spoke Pointers	10	Bottom Suage
3	Bolt Cutters	11	Top "
1	Pair Clippers	2	Set Hammers
1	Floor Plane	4	Sledge "
8	Augers	4	Clevers
6	Saws	8	Handle Punchers
5	Monkey Wrench	2	Tire Bender
3	Tri Squares	1	Sponge
7	New Bits — 14 Old ones	3	Paint Brushes
8	Twist Bits (3 broken)	2	Tire Shrinkers
1	Level	2	Forge (1 needs repair)
1	Thumb Screw	16	prs. Tongs (1 broken)
2	Spoke Shavers	1	Mandell
3	Clamps	1	Iron Horse
4	Hand Hammers	1	Grinding Stone
3	Soldering Iron	1	Miter Box

Boarding Department 1906.

11 Wash bowls.
12 Water pitchers.
12 Soap dishes.
12 Lamps.
12 Lamp wicks
12 Lamp burners.
12 Lamp chimneys
5 Chambers & lids
8 Brooms.

Dining Room

6 Silver tea spoons.
5 Silver table spoons.

6 Silver knives.
6 Silver forks.
12 Steel knives.
12 Steel forks.
12 Tin tea spoons
12 Saucers.
12 Tea cups.
10 Individual butter dishes.
1 Butter dish.
17 Dessert saucers
12 large 6 small.
3 Crackers plates.
1 Gravy bowl
1 Chipped cream pitcher pitcher
2 small milk pitcher
1 plain, 1 gilt edge
1 Sugar bowl

A.L.DS Farm in acct with B. Smith Shop   Dr.   Cr.

Date	Item	Dr.	Cr.
Dec. 30	Am't bro't forw'd	23	65
	Bolt for farm		10
	T. Joint for shovel		25
1915		1	50
Jan. 20	1 Pr Rake Shafts	2	00
" "	Shoeing		
" 25	1 Shoulder hooks		15
Feb. 4	Fixed farm wagon	1	50
	made 1 hadidle for Cleaver		20
	Put in Stove for Mrs.		
	Collins (School)		20
" 6	Filie hangers for farm		80
" 8	1 lap ring for farm		10
" 9	Filled one log wagon	3	50
	wheel for (1891)		75
	Fixed Cart		
" 10	made 8 hoe handles	1	20
" 11	Single-tree fixed 10 Lapring's Nuy		20
	pr of Strechers		25
" 15	Cleaver handle put on		25
" 18	nuts & bolts		20
" 19	Repair log wagon		50
Mch 2	bolt		10
" 4	Coupling pool bolled		20
" "	bolts put in wagon bed		15
" 16	wheel drilled & bolted		25
" 27	Shoeing	4	00
" "	Wagon repaired	25	00
Apr. 5	Log wagon wheel filled	3	50
" 2	6 2x½ bit ½ bolts & washers	1	00
" 9	4 36" x ½ bolts & washers		80
" 18	Single-tree fixed		15
" 27	Repair on derk		20
" 27	Corn drill repaired		25
		71	70

117

THE ANTI COLORING BOOK ®
of Masterpieces
Susan Striker

An Owl Book

HOLT, RINEHART and WINSTON   New York

To Jill and Robbie

*"To create forms means to live. Are not
the children who construct directly
from the secrets of their emotions
more creative than the imitators of
Greek form?"*

—August Macke

Copyright © 1982 by Susan Glaser Striker
All rights reserved, including the right to reproduce this
book or portions thereof in any form.
Published by Holt, Rinehart and Winston,
383 Madison Avenue, New York, New York 10017.
Published simultaneously in Canada by
Holt, Rinehart and Winston of Canada, Limited.

ISBN: 0-03-057874-4

First Edition

Printed in the United States of America
10 9 8 7 6 5 4 3 2 1

Many thanks to Mary Doherty, Miranda Haydn, and Anita Duquette for their
invaluable assistance.

Grateful acknowledgment is made for use of the following:
"The Great Figure" from *Collected Earlier Poems* of William Carlos Williams.
Copyright 1938 by New Directions Publishing Corporation. Reprinted by
permission of New Directions.

The Anti–Coloring Book is a registered trademark of Susan Striker.

ISBN 0-03-057874-4

Introduction

In art, there is rarely a "right" or "wrong." The artist makes choices based on mood, available materials, and personal preference. Should the color be blue or green? Should the shape be oval or round? Should the portrait show the subject smiling or not? How should objects be arranged? Each decision an artist makes determines how the finished work will look.

What if some of the decisions were different? What if *you* could decide how a masterpiece would be completed, instead of the artist who actually painted it? How would your own taste, your choices, your mood affect the way it turned out? *The Anti–Coloring Book of Masterpieces* gives you a chance to find out. It includes 38 works of art—some thousands of years old, some very recent—with part of the original missing from each one, for you to fill in.

Artists have traditionally looked to the old masters for inspiration. Sometimes an artist will copy a masterpiece exactly, to learn more about how it was painted; or an artist might pay respect to an older masterpiece by using the same subject and arrangement of objects, but painting in his or her own personal style; or occasionally one artist may parody another's painting. Great works of art give us something to think about. They inspire us to see the world from a new perspective.

Every work of art is a personal statement by the artist. You and the original artist will bring different backgrounds, experience, and materials to a work of art. It is clear from the example below, for instance, that the painter Paul Cézanne and eleven-year-old John Mengel—who had never seen the completed original before starting on his own imaginary visit to a clockmaker's home—had different ideas about how the interior should look. Perhaps if Cézanne had had magic markers his palette would also have been brighter.

In using this book, please do not look at how the original work was completed until you have finished your drawing as you want to. Remember this:

YOU ARE THE ARTIST

Whatever you draw or paint with enthusiasm, with freedom to express yourself without fear of ridicule, makes you the equal of any other great artist.

This book is intended primarily to stimulate the imagination of young artists. While working with my students on some of these pages, however, I was delighted to discover an unintended bonus. Children became very curious about whatever work of art they were completing. They began asking questions about the artist, expressed strong opinions about how the original work compared to their own, and, I later found out, did additional research in the public library. One boy proudly brought art books to school to show me how much better his picture was than the original by ''that weirdo Dali.''

It is my hope, then, that this book will not only foster creativity and expose budding artists of all ages to a variety of styles and periods, but also open a door to the wonder and endless richness of art history.

Lightly Touching uses geometric shapes to express the artist's emotions. How would you finish it to show your feelings?

Picasso painted The Charnel House because he was upset by what he read in the newspaper. Has any event made you want to draw?

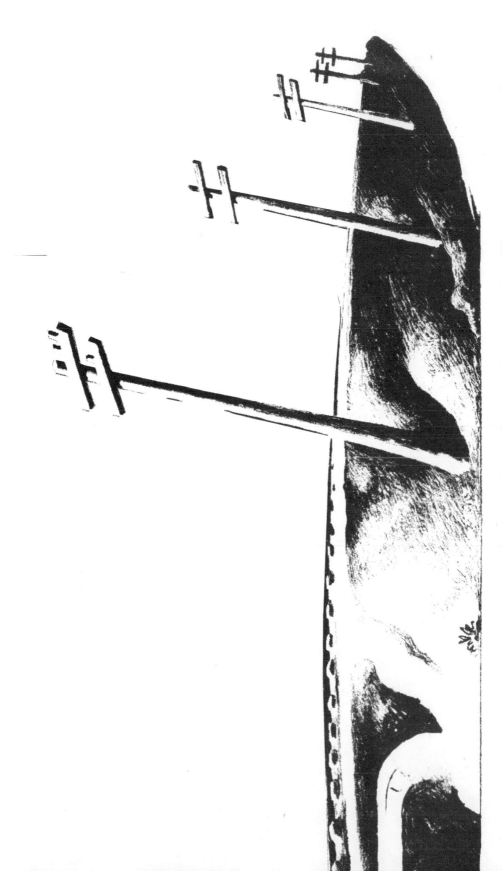

A train comes along this track once a day. Here it comes now!

Sometimes it can be fun to work so quickly you don't think about the final results until you've finished.

The artist who did Free Form dripped and splashed paint all over the canvas. Let loose and have fun!

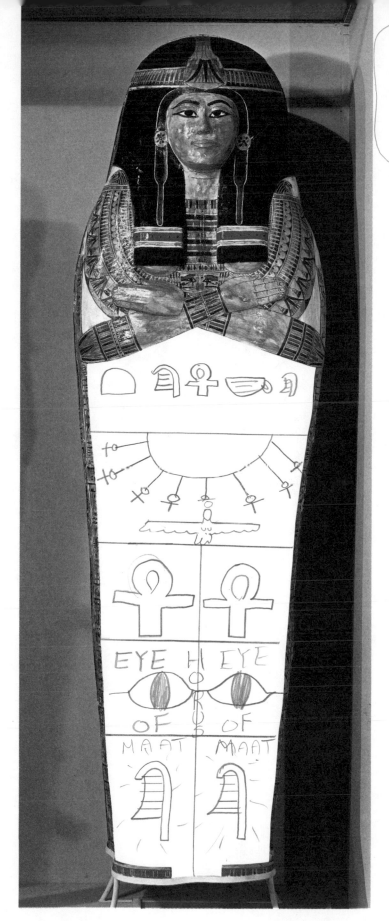

How would you have decorated Henttowe's coffin if you were a priest in ancient Egypt?

A raging storm at sea illustrated this manuscript page
from a prayer book.

This woman is famous for her mysterious smile.

Velázquez painted his daughter busy at work. What do you think she was creating?

What is the wise Greek philosopher Aristotle thinking about?

What would be interesting enough to make this man look up from his book?

This is a picture of a young boy with all his pets.

What is on the other
side of these bars?

Provide Degas' ballerinas with a stage set.

If Cézanne's father were reading a newspaper written and illustrated by you, how would this painting look?

Madame Charpentier is relaxing with her family in their home.

What do you imagine is happening while the gypsy sleeps?

*This is Mary Cassatt's sister Lydia at the garden in their summer home.
What do you think she is knitting?*

Would you like to use binoculars to see a close-up view of an exciting event?

Van Gogh painted this portrait against a background of wallpaper.

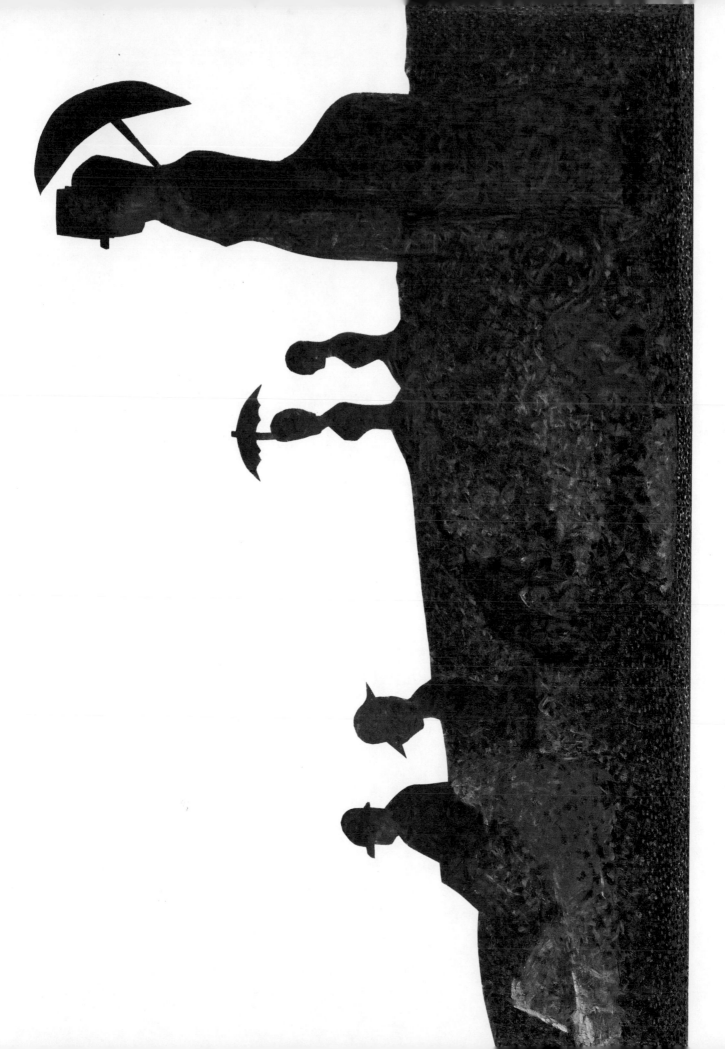

These people are watching everyone spend an afternoon in the park.

What is outside the window of Bonnard's *Breakfast Room*?

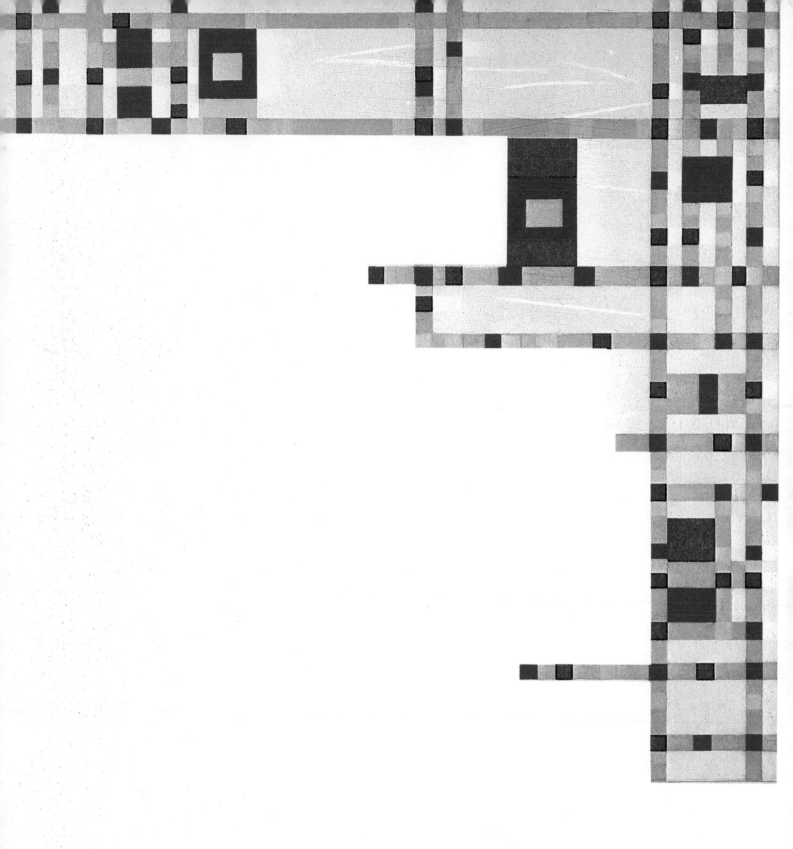

Do the shapes and colors in *Broadway Boogie Woogie* remind you of jazz?

What do you think this woman sees when she looks in the mirror?

The subject of this painting is a number. What number is it, and what do you think the rest of the picture should look like?

Who or what else is in the barnyard with Milton Avery's White Rooster?

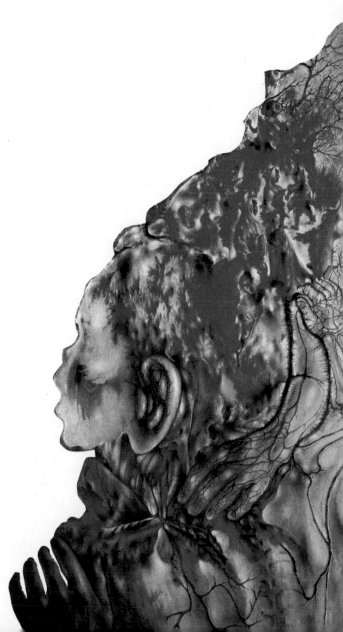

Can you imagine why Pavel Tchelitchew called
this painting *Hide-and-Seek*?

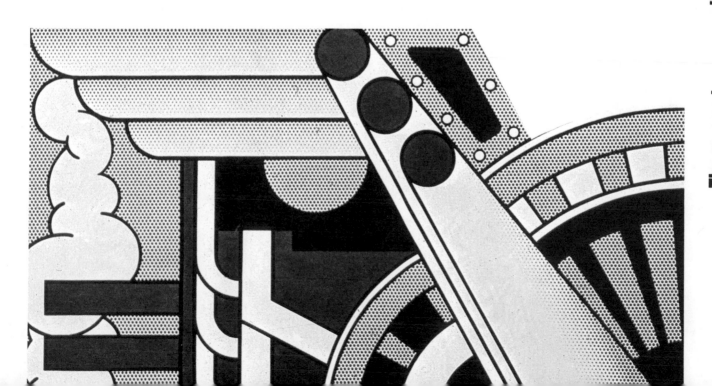

These are two panels in a three-part painting about the machine age by Roy Lichtenstein. How would you fill in the missing panel?

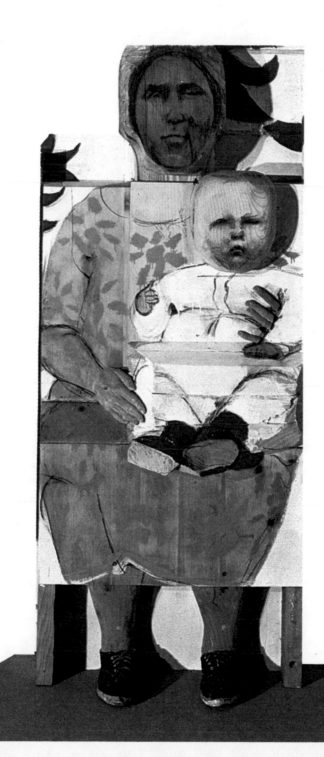

If these are the mother and baby in Marisol's assemblage _Family_, what do you think the rest of the group looks like?

The picture on this vase shows athletes practicing.

***This* City of Ambition *is seen through the creative lens of*
*Alfred Stieglitz's camera.***

Where are the horses taking this man on a cold, dreary November evening?

This is Calder's playful idea of what a person can look like.

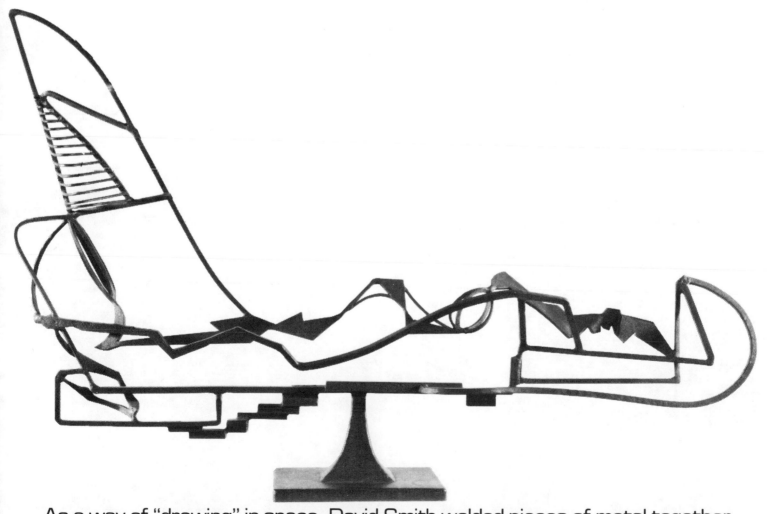

As a way of "drawing" in space, David Smith welded pieces of metal together to create *Hudson River Landscape*.

You can complete a collage by pasting paper and other materials onto the background. How would you finish Marca-Relli's collage?

Can you just imagine what the rest of the team looks like?

Bridget Riley's *Current* is inspired by wave patterns on the water and can play tricks on your eyes.

About the Masterpieces

WASSILY KANDINSKY. *Lightly Touching.* 1931.
Oil on cardboard, 27⅝ × 19¼″.
The Sidney and Harriet Janis Collection.
Gift to The Museum of Modern Art, New York.

Wassily Kandinsky (1866–1944), one of the originators of abstract art, felt that art must express something of the artist's personality. Born in Moscow, he helped found the Academy of Arts and Sciences there in 1921. The following year he went to Germany and worked at the famous Bauhaus, an influential school that experimented with abstract and modern art and architecture, becoming its president for a year. When his art was condemned by the Nazis as "degenerate," he fled to Paris.

    Lightly Touching is typical of Kandinsky's Bauhaus period, which lasted from 1922 to 1932. During that time he concentrated on the theme of the circle, square, and triangle. In this picture, tension is created by the fact that only the edges of the shapes in the painting touch. No shapes overlap or fit together.

PABLO PICASSO. *The Charnel House.* 1944–45.
Oil and charcoal on canvas, 6′ 6⅝″ × 9′ 2½″.
Collection. The Museum of Modern Art, New York.
Acquired through the Mrs. Sam A. Lewisohn
Bequest, Mrs. Marya Bernard in memory
of her husband, Dr. D. Bernard, and
anonymous funds.

Most of Pablo Ruiz y Picasso's (1881–1973) paintings were inspired by his personal experience, but *The Charnel House*, like his famous *Guernica*, is an exception. Both paintings were reactions to the horrors of war.

    Picasso did this painting after viewing newspaper photographs of concentration camps in 1944. Like the photographs, the painting is done entirely in black and white. It shows a pile of dead bodies in a room that also contains a table with food on it. In the pile of bodies one can find the figures of a man, woman, and child. The man's hands are tied behind his back like an animal about to be slaughtered. The people are wounded and suffering, while the meal on the table suggests that someone may uncaringly sit down to eat, back turned on the suffering of the victims. Flames in the upper-right-hand corner remind us of the people who died by fire in the crematoriums of the concentration camps during World War II.

THOMAS HART BENTON. *Express Train.* 1924.
Lithograph, 12¹¹/₁₆ × 23¼″.
Collection of The Whitney Museum of
American Art, New York.
Photograph by Geoffrey Clements.

Thomas Hart Benton (1889–1975) was born in Neosho, Missouri. His father was a congressman. When he was a child, Benton loved drawing Indians and trains.

He worked as a draftsman and painted scenes showing daily life in America. Because his paintings reflected his rural background in a small American town, he was considered a "regionalist" painter. Benton's work was inspired by history, folklore, and the everyday lives of common people.

FRANZ KLINE. *Painting Number 2.* 1954.
Oil on canvas, 6′ 8½″ × 8′ 9″.
Collection, The Museum of Modern Art, New York.
Mr. and Mrs. Joseph H. Hazen and
Mr. and Mrs. Francis F. Rosenbaum funds.

Along with Jackson Pollock and Willem de Kooning, Franz Kline (1910–1962) was a leading Abstract Expressionist painter. These artists used the physical act of painting to express their personal feelings. The most significant and influential style to emerge from the 1940s and 1950s, Abstract Expressionism was the first major breakthrough in painting to originate in the United States. With its development, the center of the art world moved from Paris to New York.

Franz Kline's most important paintings were quite large, and after 1950 he painted almost everything entirely in black and white. Although *Painting Number 2* appears to be completely spontaneous, Kline usually made many sketches before doing a painting. He executed the paintings themselves very quickly. Some of them have been compared to oriental calligraphy. Of his characteristic black images on white canvas he said: "I kept simplifying the forms in black and white and breaking down the structure into essential elements." Kline disagreed with critics who said his works relied on their emotional impact. When he died at the height of his career, he left the world a legacy of many paintings which were, by his own standards, great "whether or not the painter's emotion comes across."

JACKSON POLLOCK. *Free Form.* 1946.
Oil on canvas, 19¼ × 14″.
The Sidney and Harriet Janis Collection. Gift to
The Museum of Modern Art, New York.

Jackson Pollock (1912–1956) stopped doing realistic paintings in 1945 and developed Action Painting, which depended on his subconscious. Tacking canvases as large as twenty feet wide onto the floor, and working in a kind of rhythmic frenzy, Pollock threw, splashed, and dripped enamel and aluminum paints. He said:

> This way I can walk around it, work from the four sides and literally be *in* the painting. . . . When I am *in* my painting, I'm not aware of what I'm doing. It is only after a sort of "get acquainted" period that I see what I have been about. I have no fears about making changes, destroying the image, etc., because the painting has a life of its own. I try to let it come through.

Although imitated by many lesser artists and ridiculed by the public, Pollock brought to his work a wildness and freedom, yet he never lost control of it. This combination produced the fluid lines that are instantly recognizable as his. Pollock became one of the most important and influential Abstract Expressionists.

Outer and inner coffin of Henttowe.
Wood. From Thebes, Deir al-Bahri.
The Metropolitan Museum of Art, New York.
Museum Excavations, 1923–24.
Rogers Fund, 1925.

Queen Pharaoh Henttowe was only twenty-one years old when she died during the Twenty-first Dynasty (1085–950 B.C.) in ancient Egypt. She was buried in a tomb that had originally held another coffin but was plundered. Wrapped in linen and holding personal possessions such as jewelry, Henttowe was buried in this wooden coffin decorated with paint, gold, and semiprecious stones. The coffin was discovered at Deir al-Bahri, Egypt, where other ancient artifacts of high quality have been found. The fine artwork being done during the time of Henttowe included gold masks, silver coffins, jewels, and utensils used in royal and aristocratic burials.

POL, JEAN, and HERMAN DE LIMBOURG. *The Belles Heures of Jean, Duke of Berry.*
Folio 168: "St. Nicholas Stops the Storm at Sea."
c. 1406–09. Ink, tempera, and gold leaf on parchment, 9⅜" × 6⅝".
The Metropolitan Museum of Art, New York. The Cloisters Collection, purchase, 1954.

This medieval book of hours is a private prayer book illustrated in the early fifteenth century by three brothers, Pol, Jean, and Herman de Limbourg. The work was commissioned by Jean d'Evreaux, Duke of Berry, whose family was noted for its interest in art and who provided the brothers with financial security, a creative work environment, and the encouragement to be original. Such books got their name from the fact that the prayers in them were arranged according to the seven hours of the day when they were to be recited by the worshiper. This book of hours is considered by many to be the greatest example of the courtly art of France. Its drawings are excellent and the decorations are unusual and exciting.

Folio 168 shows Nicholas, Bishop of Myra and patron saint of sailors, who was famous during his lifetime for suddenly appearing when people needed help. Although it was uncommon to represent wind and stormy weather in paintings of this period, here a boat caught in a storm is about to capsize. The passengers appear to have given up hope; they do not yet know that St. Nicholas is about to rescue them.

LEONARDO DA VINCI. *Mona Lisa (La Giaconda).* c. 1503–05.
Oil on poplar panel, 30¼ × 20⅞".
The Louvre, Paris. Photograph Musées Nationaux.

Leonardo da Vinci (1452–1519) was the ultimate Renaissance man. He was a modern thinker who did not live by tradition or superstition but by observation and experience.

At the age of thirteen Leonardo was apprenticed to the artist Verrocchio, with whom he studied painting, sculpture, goldsmithing, and draftsmanship. An accomplished musician, poet, architect, and engineer, he carried out scientific experiments in anatomy, geology, botany, and other fields in order to become a better painter. His most important contribution to painting was his work with chiaroscuro, the use of dark shadows and strongly contrasting light to express a mood dramatically.

Leonardo was a great intellectual who felt that painting should not be merely decorative. *Mona Lisa* is an example of the way he encouraged viewers to think about as well as look at his work. Mona Lisa's smile has made the painting one of the most famous in the world. The viewer can interpret her expression many different ways. One is always tempted to return to it and ponder.

DIEGO VELAZQUEZ. *The Needlewoman.* c. 1640.
Oil on canvas, 29⅛ × 23⅝".
The National Gallery of Art, Washington, D.C. Andrew Mellon Collection, 1937.

The Needlewoman by Diego Rodríguez de Silva y Velázquez (1599–1660) is a portrait of his daughter, Francesca, engaged in the humble activity of sewing. It is an unusual subject for Velázquez, since most of his artwork had either a religious or a classical theme. The silvery light is typical of Velázquez's work, and the composition is arranged to emphasize the woman's busy hands.

Velázquez's portraits are noted for their great insight into the sitter's personality. He and Goya are considered the greatest Spanish portraitists of all time.

REMBRANDT HARMENSZ VAN RYN. *Aristotle with a Bust of Homer.* 1653.
Oil on canvas, 56½ × 53¾".
The Metropolitan Museum of Art, New York.
Purchased with the special funds and gifts of friends of the museum, 1961.

Dutch Baroque painting, with its meticulous details and delightful subjects, might be considered merely charming if it were not for the grandeur brought to it by the work of Rembrandt van Ryn. Rembrandt painted with the precision required by the times, but his genius at arranging space, portraying three dimensions, and using light dramatically set him apart from his contemporaries. His work involves its viewers personally and evokes strong emotions.

Rembrandt was misunderstood in his lifetime (1606–1669), alternately famous and ignored. He lost his home and collection of paintings when he was declared bankrupt in 1656. Now he is probably the most widely admired old master.

Between 1652 and 1663 Rembrandt did three paintings of great people of the world. In addition to *Aristotle with a Bust of Homer,* symbolizing poetry, he also painted *Alexander the Great* (representing philosophy) and *Homer Instructing Two of His Followers* (symbolizing poetry). Rembrandt dressed Aristotle in a gold costume rather than in authentic robes of the period, probably because he preferred the costume he saw in his imagination to one that would have been historically correct. Aristotle's sleeves are bathed in light, and they direct attention to the most important features of the painting: Aristotle's thoughtful face and the statue. All other details of the picture fade into the background.

AERT DE GELDER. *The Rest on the Flight into Egypt.* c. 1690.
Oil on canvas, 43¼ × 46½".
Courtesy, The Museum of Fine Arts, Boston.
Maria T. B. Hopkins Fund.

Aert de Gelder (1645–1727), who painted mostly biblical subjects and portraits, studied with Rembrandt in the 1660s. His scenes from the New Testament, such as *Rest on the Flight into Egypt,* are done in warm colors and have a glow and technique that make the viewer think immediately of that great Dutch master. But since the younger Gelder lived nearly sixty years beyond Rembrandt's death, his work also reflects later styles, such as Rococo, and his colors are slightly lighter.

FRANCISCO DE GOYA. *Don Manuel Osorio de Zuñiga.* c. late 1780s.
Oil on canvas, 50 × 40".
The Metropolitan Museum of Art, New York.
Jules S. Bache Collection, 1949.

Francisco José de Goya y Lucientes (1746–1828) was born in Spain but lived the last years of his life in France. As was the custom during these times, Goya decided on his life's career by the time he was fourteen and was apprenticed to an artist to study painting and assist the artist in his studio.

Goya is considered one of the most important portrait painters in the history of art, and he is also noted for his studies exploring violence and savagery in human beings.

This portrait by Goya is of four-year-old Don Manuel Osorio de Zuñiga. The child is shown wearing red trousers, a white frilled collar, and white shoes. He is holding a string tied to a bird. In the bird's beak is an engraved card which also shows the artist's signature. With Don Manuel are three cats and a birdcage containing several small birds.

EDOUARD MANET. *Gare St.-Lazare.* 1873.
Oil on canvas, 36¾ × 45⅛".
The National Gallery of Art, Washington, D.C.
Gift of Horace Havemeyer in memory of his mother, Louisine W. Havemeyer.

Edouard Manet (1832–1883) was born in France to a conservative, wealthy family who opposed his choice of a career as an artist. But his father finally let him attend the Ecole des Beaux-Arts and helped support him.

Manet studied with Thomas Couture and learned a great deal about handling tones from his teacher, who objected to his free style of painting. After leaving Couture's studio, he painted *Déjeuner sur l'Herbe (Luncheon on the Grass)* and *Olympia.* Both of these pictures were based on classic Renaissance paintings, yet the way Manet treated them, combining boldly staring nude women with clothed models, scandalized people at the time.

Manet's free brushwork, flat forms, strong contrast of light and dark, and fresh new interpretation of the old masters paved the way for the Impressionist style of painting that dominated the art world through the late nineteenth and early twentieth centuries.

EDGAR DEGAS. *The Curtain Call (Danseuse au bouquet, saluant sur la scène).* c. 1877.
Pastel, 29½ × 30¾".
The Louvre, Musée de l'Impressionnisme, Paris.

Hilaire Germain Edgar Degas (1834–1917) was a French Impressionist whose favorite subjects were dancers and racehorses. He began painting ballet dancers in 1873 and the following year showed his work in the First Impressionist Exhibition. Critics ridiculed his paintings—as well as those of other Impressionists—and the public was hostile. But since Degas had a private income, he did not have to depend on popularity to continue painting.

Degas wrote, "Drawing is not what one sees, but what one must make others see." He made his viewers see the beauty of women posed naturally in fleeting moments—while bathing, working, dressing, or relaxing. His arrangements are asymmetrical; most of his subjects are shown from an unusual viewpoint. In *The Curtain Call*, the light cast upward on the curtseying dancer's face, the casual clusters of dancers in the background with their attention directed to the side, and the sketchy partial figure of the dancer walking onstage (far left) all contribute to a feeling of naturalness, of one brief instant captured in its informal beauty.

PAUL CEZANNE. *The Artist's Father.* 1886.
Oil on canvas, 78⅛ × 47".
The National Gallery of Art, Washington, D.C.
Collection of Mr. and Mrs. Paul Mellon.

Paul Cézanne (1839–1906) was a French painter important in the Impressionist movement. He was particularly interested in the essential geometric forms of things he painted, and his later work became increasingly abstract. In fact, his paintings had a great influence on the development of Cubism.

One subject Cézanne liked to paint was his father, who posed for three paintings and many drawings. They had a difficult relationship but the elder Cézanne supported his son, even though he did not understand Paul's work. The father owned a bank, where he wanted Paul to work, but Paul was very unhappy there and thought only of painting. Finally his father gave him an allowance so that he could continue working in the field of art.

In *The Artist's Father*, Cézanne has painted the subject in a way that makes him look very solid and sturdy, almost like a sculpture. Although his large, weighty form suggests the father figure and impressive bank president, his posture and expression betray the artist's tenderness, which did not always show when they were together.

PIERRE AUGUSTE RENOIR. *Madame Charpentier and Her Children.* 1878.
Oil on canvas. 60½ × 74⅞".
The Metropolitan Museum of Art, New York.
Wolfe Fund, 1907.
Catharine Lorillard Wolfe Collection.

Pierre Auguste Renoir (1841–1919) showed artistic talent as a youngster and was apprenticed to a porcelain manufacturer, for whom he decorated plates. He later studied at the Ecole de Beaux-Arts in Paris, where he met artists Claude Monet, Frédéric Bazille, and Alfred Sisley. He and his fellow artists, called Impressionists, explored the effects of changing light on a subject and painted outdoors rather than in a studio. Renoir's paintings were done in a lively, lyrical style, and he used bright colors and free brushstrokes.

Madame Charpentier and Her Children was a great opportunity for Renoir to publicize his work. Madame Charpentier was well known in intellectual circles in Paris, and, to please her, when the painting was exhibited in the Salon the following year, it was hung in an important spot.

The picture shows Madame Charpentier seated in her luxurious home and wearing a gown by Worth, a leading dress designer of the time. Renoir painted the gown as well as other parts of the picture in black, which he considered "the queen of colors." The child sitting on the sofa is a three-year-old boy—not a girl, as many people think. His name was Paul, and he died at the age of twenty in a war. Georgette, the little girl on the dog's back, was six years old.

HENRI ROUSSEAU. *The Sleeping Gypsy.* 1897.
Oil on canvas, 51 × 79".
Collection, The Museum of Modern Art, New York.
Gift of Mrs. Simon Guggenheim.

Henri Julien Félix Rousseau (1844–1910) began painting when he was about forty years old, even while he contined to work full-time as a French customs officer. Although he never formally studied art, he copied old masters in the Louvre museum and was a friend of many artists, such as Robert Delaunay, Maurice Vlaminck, Paul Gauguin, and Pablo Picasso.

The Sleeping Gypsy, one of his best-known works, depicts a frightening dream. Rousseau is called a "primitive" painter because of the simplicity of his style, but his skillful paintings indicate that he was not ignorant of many of the principles of fine arts despite his lack of formal education in that field.

MARY CASSATT. *Lydia Crocheting in the Garden at Marly.*
1880.
Oil on canvas, 26 × 37".
The Metropolitan Museum of Art,
New York. Gift of Mrs. Gardner
Cassatt, 1965.

MARY CASSATT. *At the Opera.* 1879.
Oil on canvas, 31½ × 25½".
Courtesy, The Museum of Fine Arts, Boston.
Charles Henry Hayden Fund.

The only woman who achieved recognition as an Impressionist painter was Mary Cassatt (1845–1926). An American, she lived and worked in France for many years in the late nineteenth century, when Impressionism was at its peak. She worked closely with Degas, who greatly influenced her. Impressionists showed interest in common events of everyday life, generally used free brushstrokes, and were fascinated with the effects of changing light and color. Cassatt's favorite subjects were women as they went about their daily lives, and her affection for them and their children shows in her work. She painted women caring for babies, reading, visiting the opera, and dressing for the day.

Lydia Crocheting in the Garden at Marly is in keeping with Cassatt's interest in this subject. It portrays her sister sitting in the garden of their summer home. *At the Opera* is one of many paintings she did of an opera setting. Both pictures show Cassatt's free brushstroke, an interesting composition with strong diagonals that pull the viewer's attention to the main subject, and the overall softness of her art.

VINCENT VAN GOGH. *La Berceuse* (or
Woman Rocking a Cradle). 1888–89.
Oil on canvas, 36¼ × 28¾".
Collection, State Museum Kröller-Müller, Otterlo,
The Netherlands.

Vincent van Gogh (1853–1890) painted *La Berceuse* (or *Woman Rocking a Cradle*) in 1888–89. It is one of many portraits he did of Madame Roulin, the wife of his friend the postman. In three months in 1889 he painted her five times.

The subject is fat, has orange hair, and wears a bright green dress that contrasts strongly with the red chair she is sitting in. The yellow cord of a cradle she is holding in her hands emphasizes the strong attachment between a mother and her child. In fact, the sitter may have symbolized motherhood to van Gogh. The horizon line lies on two different levels, and reminds one of the rocking of the cradle.

As an Expressionist painter, van Gogh projected his own feelings into his paintings of objects, people, and landscapes. He painted in bright, pure colors and used strong color contrasts to evoke emotional responses from the viewer.

Van Gogh shot himself fatally while in a mental asylum, and it is easy to see how troubled he was by studying his later paintings. He did revealing portraits and self-portraits, still-lifes, and powerful, vibrant landscapes. His work had a great influence on painters in the twentieth century, and the tragic story of his life and death has captured the imagination of many people.

GEORGES SEURAT. *A Sunday Afternoon at the Grande Jatte.* c. 1884.
Oil on canvas, 27⅞ × 41⅛".
The Metropolitan Museum of Art, New York.
Bequest of Samuel A. Lewisohn, 1951.

Georges Seurat (1859–1891), a French painter, had an extremely intellectual approach to his art and made scientific studies of the effects of color and light on the eye. The way he painted was methodical and painstaking. He applied color to a canvas in small, round dots of equal size. He chose color combinations scientifically based upon the effects they had on each other and the impression they made on the eye. Close up, his paintings seem to be individual colored dots, but the human eye mixes the dots and the viewer sees the right colors and shapes of objects when standing farther away from the painting.

This painting of *A Sunday Afternoon at the Grande Jatte* is a preliminary sketch he made before finishing the final, larger version that now hangs in the Art Institute of Chicago. The Grande Jatte is an island near a suburb of Paris where the people of Paris go on summer weekends to fish, row boats, and relax along the Seine River.

PIERRE BONNARD. *The Breakfast Room.* c. 1930–31.
Oil on canvas, 62⅞ × 44⅞".
Collection, The Museum of Modern Art, New York.
Given anonymously.

This interior by Pierre Bonnard (1867–1947), with blue and pink patterned wallpaper, various bright objects, and purple shadows, is alive with color. *The Breakfast Room* was done with short brushstrokes to show the shimmery effect of the light. The composition is symmetrical, which was unusual for this period, and the diagonal lines of the tablecloth and curtains lead one's attention to the view beyond the window. This intimate look at an interior has a sense of privacy and warmth that illustrates why the style of painting used by Bonnard was called Intimist.

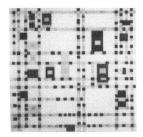

PIET MONDRIAN. *Broadway Boogie Woogie.* 1942–43.
Oil on canvas, 50 × 50".
Collection, The Museum of Modern Art, New York.
Given anonymously.

In 1917 Piet Mondrian (1872–1944) helped found the De Stijl movement of painters and architects in Holland. These painters emphasized clarity and order in their art by using straight lines, right angles, and primary colors (red, yellow, and blue). Their work symbolized human dominance over the random forms of nature.

Broadway Boogie Woogie, Mondrian's last painting, was unfinished when he died. It is complicated and vibrant; its colors and lines seem to move on the canvas, reflecting the fast pace of American urban life. Mondrian used adhesive tape to block out his composition and help him keep his lines straight, and some pieces of tape remain on the painting.

PABLO PICASSO. Girl Before a Mirror. 1932.
Oil on canvas, 64 × 51¼".
Collection, The Museum of Modern Art, New York. Gift of
Mrs. Simon Guggenheim.

Pablo Ruiz y Picasso (1881–1973) was enormously talented and extremely hard-working, and he had a very powerful personality. This rare combination made him the most important and influential artist of the twentieth century. He achieved more popular acclaim and wealth in his lifetime than any other artist ever has. He worked in many different styles and media and originated much of what is unique about this century's art. Many important artists are indebted to him for his influence on their work.

With its bright colors and strongly outlined geometric shapes, Girl Before a Mirror looks like stained glass. It is a portrait of a young woman named Marie-Thérèse Wilter. Picasso's love for Marie-Thérèse marked a turning point in his style. After he met her, he began painting in livelier colors, using more full, rounded shapes than he had earlier. Here, the subject's beauty shows in half the painting, but her image in the mirror changes to something ugly. The style of the mirror is called, in French, psyche, which is also the Greek word for "soul." Picasso may have intended this painting to represent a popular superstition that a mirror has magical properties and can reflect the soul of the person looking into it.

CHARLES HENRY DEMUTH. I Saw the Figure 5 in Gold. 1928.
Oil on composition board, 36 × 29¾".
The Metropolitan Museum of Art, New York. Alfred Stieglitz
Collection, 1949.

Born in Pennsylvania, Charles Henry Demuth (1883–1935) was one of the pioneers of the modern-art movement in the United States. His paintings—cold, geometric interpretations of the industrial world—have great strength, yet are also light and delicate. Demuth originated a style of painting known as the "poster portrait."

I Saw the Figure 5 in Gold, considered by many to be his most important painting, was inspired by a poem by William Carlos Williams, who was a close friend of his.

The Great Figure

Among the rain
and lights
I saw the figure 5
in gold
on a red
firetruck
moving
tense
unheeded
to gong clangs
siren howls
and wheels rambling
through the dark city

MILTON AVERY. *White Rooster.* 1947.
Oil on canvas, 61½ × 50¾".
The Metropolitan Museum of Art, New York. Gift of
Joyce Blaffer von Bothmer, 1975.

Milton Avery was a New Yorker who lived from 1893 to 1965. He is best known for being an important link in American art between such European color masters as Matisse and the abstract color-field painters of the 1960s, such as Mark Rothko.

During the 1940s Avery developed a style which, while abstract, always contained a recognizable subject. His works, with their large, flat areas of color, were quite different from the Social Realist style popular during that period. This barnyard scene, *White Rooster*, is typical of his art, with its soft but strong arrangements of flat, colorful shapes.

PAVEL TCHELITCHEW. *Hide-and-Seek (Cache-cache).*
1940–42.
Oil on canvas, 6' 6½" × 7' ¾".
Collection, The Museum of Modern Art, New York.
Mrs. Simon Guggenheim Fund.

Pavel Tchelitchew (pronounced Chel'-ĭ-chef) was an American painter who was born in Russia in 1898 and died in 1957. Most of his paintings showed some sort of metamorphosis—the changing of one object into another. Over eight years he did a sequence of drawings that finally became the large painting *Hide-and-Seek*. In this . symbolic picture, a gnarled tree becomes the figures of children, as the artist expressed his philosophy on the mystery of life. Art historian Alfred A. Barr, Jr., said of it: "The tree of life becomes a clock of the seasons; its greens and fiery reds and wintry blues celebrate the annual cycle of death and rebirth." Each color Tchelitchew used is also symbolic. Ocher signifies the earth and bones; green stands for lymph and water; blue indicates arteries, veins, and air; and yellow with a magenta halo symbolizes nerves and fire. Even minor details have significance in his work: the dandelion signifies "ephemeral existence and terrific tenacity."

ROY LICHTENSTEIN. *Preparedness.* 1969.
Magna on canvas, three panels,
each 120 × 72".
Collection, The Solomon R. Guggenheim
Museum, New York.
Photograph by Robert E. Mates.

Roy Lichtenstein was born in New York in 1923. His early paintings were studies of the Old West. After going through a period in which he did abstract symbolic paintings, he began in 1961 to use a shading technique known as Ben Day dots, and his main subjects became advertisements and comic strips. Throughout the 1960s he was a leader in the Pop Art movement.

Lichtenstein described this work, *Preparedness*, as a "muralesque painting about our military-industrial complex" and chose the title to suggest a call to arms. It is actually three paintings hung side by side to form a triptych, with the three panels visually unified by the diagonals of the composition. Dots and bright primary colors are used in all three panels.

The panel on the left is of the smokestacks of factories. The center panel shows a hand holding a hammer and gears and a row of soldiers. In the right-hand panel we see another soldier and the window of an airplane.

MARISOL ESCOBAR. *The Family.* 1962.
Painted wood and other materials in three sections,
82⅝ × 65".
Collection, The Museum of Modern Art, New York.
Advisory Committee Fund.

Marisol Escobar (1930–   ) was born in France but has lived in New York since 1950. A sculptor, she creates works that include painting, carving, drawing, plaster casts, and objects she has collected. Her figures or groups of figures are frequently larger than life-size, and most are comments on the values of modern society. Her work, such as this sculpture titled *The Family*, combines irony, satire, pity, and humor.

Lekythos (Greek vase). Black-figured athletes practicing.
c. 525–500 B.C.
The Metropolitan Museum of Art, New York. Rogers Fund, 1906.

During the sixth century B.C., Greek vases were made of red clay and decorated with black glaze. Because they usually showed scenes of daily life or portrayed myths, they have given us much of the information we have about Greek life during the period they were made. This vase shows athletes practicing. The ornamental design framing the scene divides the vase and decorates the areas not covered by the scene. The lotus flower and palmette in the borders were favorite decorations of the period.

ALFRED STIEGLITZ. *City of Ambition.* 1911.
Photograph.
The Metropolitan Museum of Art, New York. Alfred Stieglitz Collection, 1933.

Alfred Stieglitz (1864–1946) was a photographer as well as a gallery director and editor. As a photographer he was recognized for the freshness and originality of his vision. As an editor of photography magazines, he supported the work of other innovative photographers. In Gallery 261, which he established with Edward Steichen, he exhibited the newest and most radical examples of modern painting, architecture, and sculpture.

A pioneer of modern art, Stieglitz championed the cause of photography as the first new art form to come along in five thousand years. His own photographs were straightforward and evoked strong emotional responses.

Stieglitz was married to painter Georgia O'Keeffe. The many photographs he took of her over the years are considered to be the most comprehensive portrait ever done of one person.

CHARLES E. BURCHFIELD.
November Evening. 1934.
Oil on canvas, 32⅛ × 52''.
The Metropolitan Museum of Art,
New York.
George A. Hearn Fund, 1934.

Charles Burchfield (1893–1967), born in Ohio and educated at Cleveland School of Art, painted scenes typical of rural America and filled them with fantasy and drama. His work is admired for the way it expresses personal feelings and the tremendous power of nature. Burchfield said about *November Evening*: "I have tried to express the coming of winter over the middle-west as it must have felt to the pioneers—great black clouds sweep out of the west at twilight as if to overwhelm not only the pitiful attempt at a town, but also the earth itself."

The dark clouds, the emptiness of the town, the posture of the man and horses combine to give a sense of loneliness and isolation.

ALEXANDER CALDER. *Slanting Red Nose.* 1969.
Gouache, 29½ × 43¼″.
Collection, The Museum of Modern Art, New York.
Gift of Mr. and Mrs. Klaus G. Perls.

Alexander Calder was born in 1898 in Philadelphia and died in 1976. His father and grandfather were both sculptors, and he too is known more for his three-dimensional works than for his paintings. Calder is most famous for inventing delicately balanced sculptures that are held together by wires and move by air currents; the artist Marcel Duchamp named them "mobiles." Because they are constantly moving, these mobiles look different from moment to moment; exactly what the viewer sees as the "finished" sculpture depends on chance. Calder's use of chance as an element in sculpture influenced many other artists who followed him.

 Both his paintings and sculptures give a sense of exuberance, fantasy, and joy. Calder preferred pure reds, yellows, and blues—the primary colors—and used them with great humor and simplicity, as in this painting, *Slanting Red Nose.*

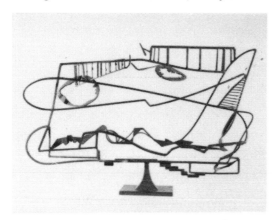

DAVID SMITH. *Hudson River Landscape.* 1951.
Steel, 49¼ × 75 × 16¾″.
Collection of The Whitney Museum of American Art, New York.
Photograph by Jerry L. Thompson.

David Smith (1906–1965) began as a Cubist painter earning his living as a metal worker, and eventually turned to sculpture. He described the transition by saying: "The painting developed into raised levels from the canvas. Gradually the canvas was the base and the painting was a sculpture." He was greatly influenced by the works of Spanish sculptor Julio González and Pablo Picasso.

 Hudson River Landscape is an example of "drawing in space." It was the first piece of open sculpture in the modern era and was intended to be viewed from the front only. Smith had no preconceived plan for it; the sculpture came to him spontaneously as he worked on it.

 Considered to be one of the most important twentieth-century sculptors, Smith was the first in America to weld in iron. He produced many works and brought a fresh, typically American vision and industrial skill to the formal, more European concepts of sculpture. He expressed his love for technology by saying: "The equipment I use, my supply of material comes from factory study, and duplicates as nearly as possible the production equipment used in making a locomotive. . . . What associations the metal possesses are those of this century: power, structure, movement, progress, suspension, destruction, brutality."

CONRAD MARCA-RELLI. *Junction.* 1958.
Collage of painted canvas, 56 × 77¼".
Collection of The Whitney Museum of American Art,
New York.
Gift of the Friends of The Whitney Museum
of American Art.
Photograph by Geoffrey Clements Photography.

Junction is a collage by Conrad Marca-Relli (1913–), who specializes in combining oil paint and collage in a large format. Born in Boston and mostly self-taught in painting technique, Marca-Relli frequently begins his work with the suggestion of a human figure, then pastes canvas scraps to the background and covers them with painted brushstrokes. The completed work is abstract, marked by free expression, and often done on a monumental scale. He is considered to be an American master of collage.

NIKI DE SAINT PHALLE. *Black Venus.* 1967.
Painted polyester, 110" × 35" × 24".
Collection of The Whitney Museum of American Art, New York.
Gift of the Howard and Jean Lipman Foundation.

Niki de Saint Phalle (1930–) is a "pop" artist born in New York City and is now living in France. She is known for her zany and humorous "Nanas"—large, exaggerated sculptures of women with tiny heads, featureless faces, targets, hearts, and flowers decorating the huge bodies. By emphasizing the body instead of the head, the artist makes amusing comment on stereotypes of women.

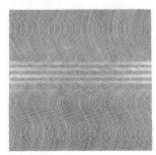

BRIDGET RILEY. *Current.* 1964.
Synthetic polymer paint on composition board,
58⅜ × 38⅞".
Collection, The Museum of Modern Art, New York.
Philip Johnson Fund.

Op Art is a kind of dynamic, graphic design that depends on visual devices and optical illusions. It became popular during the late 1960s after a major exhibit titled The Responsive Eye was held in 1965 at New York's Museum of Modern Art.

Unlike some other Op artists who have been accused of merely painting visual tricks, Bridget Riley (1931–) has consistently produced works of depth. An English member of the Op Art movement, she uses optical effects to express facets of her own personality and to interpret her impressions of natural landscapes. *Current* is an abstract interpretation of the pattern ripples make on a stream. Its close black-and-white wave pattern hits the viewer's eyes with movement and is typical of the black-and-white work she painted exclusively from 1960 to 1967.